GOOD KING WENCESLAS
~ THE REAL STORY ~

by Jan Rejzl BSc MSc

Published by
1st Choice Publishing

Published by
1st Choice Publishing Limited
St Wenceslas House
355 Aylsham Road
Norwich NR3 2RX
Great Britain

Telephone Sales: 01603 410111
Telephone Admin: 01603 404001
Facsimile: 01603 404410

A CIP catalogue record for this book
is available from the British Library

ISBN 0 9527339 0 0

Typeset and printed by
Catton Printing
13 & 14 Roundtree Close
Norwich NR7 8SX

Romanesque door knocker on the door of
St Wenceslas Chapel - reported to be the
same as the one on the door of Saints
Cosmas and Damian Church in front of
which Good King Wenceslas died.

GOOD KING WENCESLAS - THE REAL STORY
by Jan Rejzl BSc MSc

PART I - THE STORY AND LEGENDS

Introduction

PART II - PLACES OF INTEREST

PART I - THE STORY AND LEGENDS

INTRODUCTION

In the English-speaking world, the Christmas carol 'Good King Wenceslas' is well known. Every year it touches us with the warmth and generosity that is felt at this special time of the year - Christmas.

When I came to Great Britain in 1968, I was pleasantly surprised to hear the carol as I knew a little more about Good King Wenceslas. I was able to tell my friends that Good King Wenceslas really existed and that I come from the country he once ruled. Indeed, I was born and raised in the town where his brother Boleslav had his castle. The town is called Stara Boleslav, and is situated where Boleslav's castle once stood, in Central Bohemia in the Czech Republic.

Good King Wenceslas was from the Premyslid dynasty of Czech dukes and kings. He was also canonised and is recognised as a saint by the Roman Catholic Church.

I was an altar boy at the Basilica of Saint Wenceslas in Stara Boleslav, which was built over the smaller church of the Saints Cosmas and Damian, and the place where Good King Wenceslas was killed. He is more commonly known in his home country of Bohemia as Saint Vaclav. The English name Wenceslas is derived from his name in Latin: Wenceslaus; while in the modern Czech language Wenceslas is Vaclav.

I remember kneeling as an altar boy at the main altar of the Saint Wenceslas Basilica, looking at the painting in which he is guarded by two angels and not understanding why he was killed. On my way home, I imagined that the old castle buildings suddenly rose around me, but I was always in time to run to Good King Wenceslas's assistance, to fight off his assassins and save his life.

Years later in Great Britain, I used to tell my friends how much more there was to the story about Good King Wenceslas. I kept threatening that I would write a book about it but never found the time. I finished university, worked, got married, started in business and was just too busy to do it.

When I returned for the first time to Czechoslovakia in 1988, I started to visit all the places of importance, collected books, made notes and took photographs so I could write my book. After years of struggling with research of this more than thousand-year-old history and putting it down, well here it is. I hope that you will find it interesting.

1. EARLY HISTORY AND LEGENDS OF GOOD KING WENCESLAS'S LAND

Archeological finds indicate that the Bohemian basin in Central Europe was inhabited from the very early days of mankind. There are finds from the Old Stone Age (Paleolithic) through the New Stone Age (Neolithic), Bronze Age, Iron Age and the Celtic culture, which span across Europe from Scotland and Ireland as far as Bohemia. The first reported finds are from the Celtic culture in the 4th century BC. The very name of Bohemia is derived from a Celtic tribe called Boj (Boi) residing in and around today's Prague. Bohemia means in Germanic 'homeland of the Boj people'.

Before the end of the 1st century BC, the Celtic tribes fell to Germanic tribes under the leadership of Duke Marboda. Afterwards, various Germanic tribes settled in Bohemia.

At the end of the 5th century, Slavonic tribes started to move from the east and north, settling in Bohemia and further south. The whole movement of Slavonic tribes west and south over a period of time is not easily explained, as there are no records of it, just archaeological finds. The movement also depended on the movement of other nations and tribes.

Ancient long-distance European trade routes passed through Bohemia and settlements existed along the routes. One such settlement was in today's Prague, which was an important trade, craft and industrial centre well before the ducal castle was established there. It may be because of the growing importance of Prague that the Premyslid rulers of the Czech tribe decided to establish their presence.

The local culture was gradually absorbed by the newly settled Slavonic tribes of Czechs and several others. Like Croats, who inhabited White Croatia covering East Bohemia and adjoining land in today's Poland, Lusatian Serbs, inhabited today's East Germany and spilled over to North Bohemia. Other tribes that settled in Bohemia included: the Lemuzi (from the same area as Premysl came from), the Lucane, the Doudlebs in South Bohemia, the Psovane along the river Elbe and the Zlicane with their centre in Kourim.

Archeological finds indicate that the Slavonic settlements co-existed with some of the existing inhabitants. During this movement of tribes and nations, a Germanic tribe called the Durings moved on from Bohemia further west into today's Bavaria.

Of all the tribes, the Czechs managed to dominate Central Bohemia. There is a legend of how the Czech ruling dynasty of Premyslid was established. It is believed that this was passed verbally from generation to generation until it was recorded by the first Czech chronicler Cosmas in the 11th century.

The following is a translation of a legend chronicled by Cosmas, a married priest with a son, who lived between 1045 and 1125.

There was a man called Krok, among the Czech tribe, who was respected for his wealth and wisdom. Others came to him for advice or to judge their disputes. He had three daughters: the eldest, Kazi, knew all about herbs and medicine and as a doctor, helped people in their illnesses where others would have given up. The second, Tetka, built a strong castle called Tetin. She advised people about their pagan gods and indeed was their priestess. The youngest, Libuse, also built a strong castle for herself and called it Libusin. Libuse was respected for her wisdom. She was a clairvoyant - a prophetess. When their father Krok died, the people assembled and chose Libuse to be their judge.

A dispute arose between two men, who were known for their wealth and their positions of authority. The dispute, which was about a hedge between two fields, spilled into an argument and confrontation and so they went to Libuse to settle their differences. She resolved the dispute according to local law. However, the man who lost did not like the result and told her in no uncertain terms what he thought of a woman judging a men's dispute. He concluded, "It is certain that all women have long hair but are short on wisdom. It is better for men to die than to be under a woman's rule. It is only ourselves who are humiliated in front of all the other nations and tribes, that we have not got a man to rule us."

Libuse, hiding her hurt pride, managed a smile and replied to him, "Yes, it is so as you say. I am a woman and live like woman. If you have no respect for my judgment, just because I did not judge you with an iron rod and if you think that I am not wise just because I am a woman, then there will have to be a ruler, stronger and harder than a woman, for you to respect him. Go home now. Tomorrow, I will tell you whom you can choose for your duke and I will also accept him as my husband."

Libuse called upon her sisters for advice. The next day she called the people together and sitting on a very high stool she spoke to the assembled men, "People, I pity you that you cannot live freely. Let me tell you more. It will be in your power to raise a man to the status of a duke. But as soon as he becomes your duke, all that you have will be under his jurisdiction. To his orders you will only be able to answer - yes our Lord, yes our Lord. But I do not want to hold you back or unnecessarily frighten you, the choice is yours. If you still want a duke to rule you and you are not mistaken in your wish then I will tell you his name and where you will find him."

The assembled people rejoiced and shouted in one voice, asking to be given a duke.

Libuse then revealed his whereabouts and name, saying: "Look beyond these mountains," and she pointed at the mountains, "there is a small river, Bilina, and on its bank is a village, Stadice.

Fig. 1.1 Libuse judging the two men. Drawing by M. Ales

Near by, there will be your duke, ploughing a field with two oxen. Take him duke's robes and give him my message and greetings from our people and bring him back to be your duke and my husband. His name is Premysl and that name in itself means 'Thinker'."

The people were filled with joy upon learning this.

A delegation was assembled to take Libuse's request to the man. However, they were unsure which way to go and as soon Libuse saw their hesitation she told them, "Why do you hesitate? Take my horse and go without a worry. My horse will lead you to him and all the way back as it has done that journey several times."

Some people were indeed saying that Libuse herself had been undertaking this journey on her horse secretly at night and returning home before the dawn. (Cosmas, although reporting it, thought this comment to be unworthy of the Duchess Libuse.)

And so the selected group of elders went with the message from Libuse to find their duke. They followed her horse over the mountains to the village called Stadice, where nearby they found Premysl ploughing a field with a pair of oxen.

The messengers approached him and said, "Blissful man and a duke, sent to us by gods, we greet you your highness, release oxen from your plough and put on a new robe and mount your new horse." They showed him his new duke's robe and the stallion they had brought for him. They continued, "Our lady Libuse and the people send their plea that you soon come and accept the estates, which are adjudged to you and your descendants. All we have, including ourselves, is in your hands. We want you to be our duke, our judge, our steward, our defender. We choose only you to be our lord."

Premysl stopped ploughing the field, released the oxen from the plough and let them go. He then pushed his whip into the soil. The whip was made from a branch of a hazelnut bush. To the surprise of the messengers, three branches with leaves and hazelnuts sprung from the whip. Premysl asked them in a friendly manner, "Sit down and have breakfast with me." He took bread and cheese out of his bag, which was made of tree bast. He put the bag on the ground as a table, covering it with a simple linen cloth. As they ate the bread and cheese and drank water from a jug, two of the branches which had sprung from the stick, dried up and fell off. The messengers were even more surprised, but their new duke, Premysl, explained, "Let it be known that there will be many lords born in our dynasty, but only one will rule at any one time." (See fig. 1.2.)

Afterwards, Premysl dressed in his new robe, put on his new shoes as the legend tells. Then the ploughman strapped the saddle on his new stallion.

Not forgetting his origins, he took with him his sandals and the bag made from tree bast. When asked by the messengers why he was taking them with him, Premysl explained, "I want them to be kept forever so that my descendants can see proof of their humble origins. These should remind them not to oppress people, given to them by God to rule, because we are all made equal by nature."

As they approached Libuse's castle, Libuse and her people came out to meet Premysl and the party accompanying him. Libuse and Premysl were pleased to see each other and hand in hand they walked into the castle. They sat on a soft settee and refreshed themselves and celibrated their union. The rest of the night they spent in each other's arms.

The people rejoiced to have a duke. Premysl and Libuse then ruled jointly, laying down all the laws their country was governed by.

On one day, during the early days of their rule, when Libuse felt the special powers of a prophetess, she explained a vision to her husband and elders.

"I can see a castle, whose fame reaches the heaven. It is some distance away from here and one side is touched by the waves of the river Vltava. From the north it is protected by the deep valley of the stream Brusnice. To the south there is a wide rocky mountain called Petrin. Go there and build a castle called Praha (Prague). In this castle sometime in the future, two golden olives will come to being, which will reach seventh heaven by their achievements and they will shine in the whole world with their miracles. They will be respected and admired by all the generations of inhabitants of the Czech Lands and also other nations. One will be called Great Glory and the other Army Conciliation."

'Great Glory' is the Czech meaning of the name of St Wenceslas in the Old Slavonic Language while 'Army Conciliation' is the Czech meaning of the name of St Vojtech - also known as St Adalbert of Prague.

Thus we have Cosmas and his legend of how the main dynasty of Czech dukes and kings was established and how they started their rule in central Bohemia. Their dukedom developed into what became known as the Kingdom of Bohemia. Good King Wenceslas was from this dynasty. Cosmas names seven more dukes who ruled the Czech tribe after Premysl and before Borivoj, who is the first historically documented duke and was the grandfather of Good King Wenceslas.

What about other historical sources? What do they say about these early days? Besides archaeology, there are not many, as writing was not known at that time in the region. There is the first record of Samo, by the Frankish monk Fredegara in his Historia Francorum. Samo united the west Slavonic tribes in around AD623 enabling them to fight the attacking Avars. Samo himself was a Frankish merchant, but he was elected king of the Slavonic tribes in Central Europe in appreciation of his achievement in defeating the Avars. On another occasion the Slavs had to stand up to a large army of the Frankish King Dagobert. Samo's Slavonic army defeated the Franks. However, his seat and the borders of his kingdom are not known exactly. Historians indicate that the kingdom might have stretched from the Alps across Moravia and Bohemia to the former East Germany, an area which was then inhabited by Slavonic tribes. We only know that Samo ruled for thirty-five years and that by his twelve wives he had twenty-two sons and fifteen daughters. After his death, sometime in AD658-9 all news disappeared about his kingdom as it disintegrated into individual tribes and dukedoms.

Chronologically, Samo was long before Premysl, so the legend does not clash with historical sources. But F. Dvornik and other historians suggest that Premysl was already a duke of the tribe Lemuzi, settled in Bohemia and that the legend was created with time to embellish the early days of the Premyslid dynasty. But with such a distant past it is impossible to make a clear judgment and we have to accept the legend as a window into faraway times. The legend, as recorded by Cosmas, inspired artists through the centuries and the composer Bedrich Smetana wrote an opera called *Libuse* in the last century.

As time went by, significant gains were made by neighbouring Franks. Charles the Great (Charlemagne) gradually expanded his sphere of influence and was crowned by the Pope as Holy Roman Emperor in AD800. Thus he became responsible not only for the administration of the empire but also for the well-being of the Christian Church. In those days the spread of Christianity was associated with such title. In AD805 and 806, several major military expeditions led by the son of Charles the Great were made against the Slavonic tribes of Bohemia, who were pagan at that time. Thus at the end of his rule, Czech tribes in Bohemia became subordinated to Charles the Great. The form of subjugation is not clear, as Czech dukes remained in power and only provided payments to him. Elsewhere in the empire Charles the Great practised direct rule.

Christianity was first introduced to Bavaria by Irish-Scottish missionaries. Regensburg in Bavaria, as a bishop's residence, was an important centre from which missionaries spread Christianity further east to Bohemia. From Passau, Christianity spread to Moravia and from Salzburg to Slovakia. The main language of worship of the missionaries from the west was Latin.

The spread of Christianity further east had great importance for further state developments. Thus it is recorded that in AD845 fourteen Slavonic dukes were christened in Bavarian Regensburg by the bishop. Some claim they were Bohemian dukes while others argue they were from Slavonic tribes further north of Bohemia. But it is documented that Borivoj was the first known Czech duke to be baptised in Moravia around AD874.

Moravia lies south-east of Bohemia. Slavonic tribes were united in this area in the 9th century under their duke Mojmir, with their main centre of rule being in Velehrad. In AD830 Mojmir defeated Pribina, Duke of Nitra, and added Slovakia to Moravia. His successor from 846, Rostislav, further developed the state into a wealthy and independent empire. Bohemia became part of this empire, which is now known as Great Moravia, as it was referred to by the Byzantine emperor Konstantin Porfyrogenetos in his writings in the 10th century.

As the spread of Christianity from the west was also associated with political influence, Rostislav felt that he wanted his own religious administration, and his own bishop to consecrate new churches and priests. He sent messengers to the Pope in Rome, but was unsuccessful in his request, and thus in 863 he sent messengers to the Byzantine emperor, Michael III, with the request that a bishopric should be established in Moravia. Emperor Michael sent two well-educated priests, the brothers Constantine and Methodius. They were Greek by origin and from a well established merchant family. Besides being priests, they were also educated in philosophy and languages, among them the Slavonic language.

They left for Great Moravia with a considerable convoy. Constantine, who was more educated than Methodius, before leaving prepared a Slavonic alphabet, based on the Greek one, and added additional necessary letters. It was the first Slavonic alphabet, called Hlaholice (also Glagolica). He also translated the most important parts of the Bible into Hlaholice, and took them with him. Once in Moravia he continued to translate other religious books and thus Constantine and his brother, together with their pupils, formed the basis of the first Slavonic literacy.

Their celebration of the holy mass in the native language was not popular with the priests from the west who used Latin. They complained to the Pope in Rome and so the Pope called the brothers Constantine and Methodius to Rome to defend their translation of the Bible into the Slavonic language. After learned discussions, Constantine successfully defended their translation of the scriptures and he was consecrated to be the first bishop of Moravia. Constantine, however did not return with Methodius. He fell ill in Rome and entered a monastery where he took on a new name, Cyril. He died there several weeks later.

While Constantine and Methodius were in Rome, Svatopluk, a nephew of Rostislav, managed to depose his uncle Rostislav with the help of the Franks. Rostislav was blinded and imprisoned, and he later died. Methodius was also imprisoned on his way from Rome and for three years he was held in a monastery in Reichenau on Frankish territory. On the request of the Pope he was finally released and in 880 he was made an archbishop of Moravia. He died in 885 and with him died the Slavonic Christian liturgy in Moravia. Svatopluk after the death of Methodius supported Latin as the language for Christian worship and all the pupils of Cyril (Constantine) and Methodius were imprisoned and then expelled. They found their way to monasteries in Bulgaria where they contributed further to the development of the Slavonic liturgy, using the improved writing of Hlaholice: Cyrillic, named after its founder, Cyril. Cyrillic writing spread from Bulgaria west to parts of Yugoslavia and further east to Russia and the Ukraine. Cyril and Methodius were rewarded for their unblemished service to Christianity by canonisation into sainthood. They are still celebrated throughout Europe as Saints Cyril and Methodius.

As Svatopluk grew old, he realised the importance of unity among his three sons. According to a legend he once called his sons to his side and showed them three wooden sticks tied together, which he then asked each son to try to break. When they could not break all three sticks held together, he untied them and passed each son a stick asking him to try to break the individual stick on its own. As they each broke the one stick given to them, he told them that it should teach them that if they stayed united, Great Moravia would stay strong and would withstand attacks from the outside. However, if they should split up and stand on their own, they would easily be overcome by outside forces. He passed his rule to one son, Mojmir II, while he asked the other two to be subordinate and of assistance to him.

After the death of Svatopluk in 894, his fears were realised. Great Moravia was weakened by an internal struggle between the brothers. The Czech tribes of Bohemia separated from Moravia and in 895 renewed their alliance with the Franks' Empire by visiting Arnulf in Regensburg. Mojmir II, the ruler of Moravia, tried to bring Bohemia under Moravian control again by military means. However, Bohemia complained to Arnulf in 897. And when one of Svatopluk's sons, also called Svatopluk, came for help to Arnulf in his struggle against his brother Mojmir II, with the support of Bohemia Arnulf took military action in 898, 899 and 900 against Moravia.

Also around 896 Magyars settled in the low lands in the area known today as Hungary. Moravia was not able to stand up to attacks by Magyar horsemen and by 906 had disintegrated. The Magyars took Slovakia into their sphere of control permanently and it stayed like that for over 1000 years.

Bohemia, surrounded by mountains which provided a natural defence, managed to survive the collapse of Great Moravia intact and decades later added Moravia to its sphere of influence.

2. WENCESLAS IS BORN INTO A CHANGING SOCIETY

Christianity was gradually seeping into Bohemia bringing with it new beliefs, new values and a new way of life, but the change was not always easy.

Borivoj, Wenceslas's grandfather, was born around 852-3 and became the ruling duke of the Czech tribe in around 867-8, at the age of fifteen years. At the age of 21 or 22 he married Ludmila, who was then fifteen. Ludmila had been born in Melnik, in a neighbouring dukedom. By their marriage the Czech dukedom was enlarged.

Bohemia was subordinated to Svatopluk of Moravia, but there were also family ties with Moravia, as Svatopluk married Borivoj's sister. With these ties also came trade and religious influence. Borivoj, on a visit with his escort to Svatopluk in Moravia, was first very warmly welcomed, but when the main reception started, he and his men were not allowed to sit at the same table to eat their meals. Humiliatingly Borivoj's and his escort's food was laid out for them on the floor, because they were pagans and this was customary for Svatopluk. Methodius felt sorry for Borivoj and went over to explain to him the difference between Christianity and the worship of pagan gods. When Borivoj asked what was stopping him from becoming Christian, Methodius replied that nothing stood in the way, but he had to accept Christianity with his whole heart.

Methodius began to educate Borivoj and his man in the fundamentals of Christianity on the next day and after Borivoj and his thirty-strong escort undertook the customary fasting, they were then baptised with holy water into Christianity. Their conversion happened in around the year 874.

When Borivoj returned to Bohemia, Methodius sent with him a priest named Kaich, to help the spread of their new religion. Borivoj established the first church in Bohemia, a rotunda dedicated to St Clement, in the grounds of the main castle and ducal seat, Levy Hradec. Methodius followed soon after to Bohemia and he baptised Duchess Ludmila, Borivoj's wife.

But it was not easy to convince the people and soon Borivoj had to face an uprising against him led by another duke: Strojmir. Borivoj escaped to Moravia, but after a year in exile he was able to return with the help of friends.

Borivoj then established a new castle in Prague. (See fig. 2.1.) He built it on a special hill where there was a pagan altar for pagan sacrifices and also a traditional stone ducal throne for the enthronement of Czech dukes. It had been customary for these to be placed on bare hills away from settlements. Borivoj built a church dedicated to St Mary in place of the pagan altar. The traditional throne was now within the boundaries of his castle and thus Borivoj strenthened his rule. A permanent army unit of Moravian soldiers was also stationed there, as indicated by archaeological finds.

Borivoj and Ludmila helped the spread of Christianity and this influenced the way people lived. Priests from Moravia brought with them the ability to read and write in what is now referred to as the Old Slavonic Language. For the first time people were educated in reading and writing.

Plants to grow vine grapes were also brought from Moravia and the first vineyards were established. Tradition assigns this deed to Ludmila herself as one of the oldest recorded vineyards can be found near Melnik, her childhood home. But archaeological finds also indicate vine growing on the slopes of Prague Castle. Borivoj and Ludmila had two sons, Spytihnev, born in 875 and Vratislav, born in 888. Both sons were brought up as Christians by their mother Ludmila.

Borivoj died in around 888 or 889 at the age of thirty-six, while his sons were still very young. Spytihnev was nine and Vratislav was one year old. Svatopluk of Moravia took direct control over Bohemia, and this was confirmed to him by Arnulf, Duke of Bavaria. In 894, Svatopluk died leaving Spytihnev to take over at the age of nineteen. He ruled until his death at the age of forty, but left no heir.

Spitihnev too helped Christianity to spread and built a new church in Budec which was dedicated to St Peter. Budec became the first seat of learning in Bohemia. During his twenty-one-year-long rule, Spitihnev was able to build additional castles on the borders of his dukedom to strengthen its security. One such castle was in Stara Boleslav. Vratislav, under his brother's rule, assumed a secondary role, as was customary in such situations. He went on diplomatic missions abroad and took part in military excursions. On one such mission, giving military help to another Slavonic dukedom further north, situated in what was later East Germany, he met his future wife Drahomira (also Dragomir). Drahomira's father Tugumir had his main castle in a place named Stodor, on the river Havole. Vratislav married Drahomira in 906. Drahomira's people were still pagan at that time and there is no doubt that she was brought up with pagan customs and beliefs. She was most probably christened before being married to Vratislav, as would have been expected in such circumstances.

When Spitihnev was on the throne and staying in Prague Castle, Vratislav occupied castles outside Prague on the border of their dukedom. Wenceslas was born in 907 to Vratislav and his wife Drahomira in Stochov, according to folk legends.

Stochov was one of the smaller castles west of Prague. Today, there is nothing left of that castle, except a village of the same name and an oak tree which is reported to have been planted by Ludmila at the time of Wenceslas's birth. Stochov means in the Czech language 'a hundred nannies' and one legend says these nannies were in service at the time Wenceslas was born. (See fig. 2.2.) Another legend says that the nannies watered the newly planted oak tree with the bath water after they bathed young Wenceslas and thus ensured the staying powers of the tree.(See fig. 2.3.)

The name Stochov has a similiar root as Stodor, the birthplace of Wenceslas's mother Drahomira. Sto-dor means in Slavonic 'a hundred doors' which could suggest the name Sto-chov was created by Drahomira herself in the same tradition as of her birthplace Sto-dor. This and the folk legends suggest Stochov as the correct birthplace of Wenceslas, although there is no written record and some sources suggest Levy Hradec and even Stara Boleslav as the birthplace of Prince Wenceslas.

Only 5.5km away from Stochov was Libusin, a much larger castle established by the Duchess Libuse, as our first legend tells us. At Libusin was a large military unit as was appropriate for a castle on the border of the dukedom. The unit also protected cattle, and inhabitants settled around the castle for safety against the wild animals that were abundant in the adjoining forests. These ranged from brown bears and lynxes to wolves. Libusin was an important border castle but it would have been in Stochov, the smaller and quieter castle near-by that Drahomira chose to have her first child, Wenceslas, rather than in the larger and very busy Libusin. Vratislav also built a church dedicated to St George in Libusin. It is possible that it was here that Wenceslas would have been christened at an early age.

Wenceslas had two younger brothers, of whom only Boleslav survived. We can imagine the joy of Vratislav and Drahomira when their first son was born that they named him Wenceslas - meaning Great Glory, forming the name as Wenche-Slav. They must have been equally overjoyed when Boleslav was born, one or two years later (it is not known exactly how much younger he was), because they gave him a name also meaning Great Glory, but the great is derived from another Slavonic name for great - bolshoi, forming the name as Bole-Slav. The name of their third son was Spytihnev, and he is believed to have died very young. Of Wenceslas's sisters only Pribyslava is known from historical sources, although one legend says that all four were married to neighbouring dukes.

In 915, when Duke Spytihnev died at the age of forty, his brother Vratislav, the second son of Borivoj, became the ruling duke at the age of twenty-seven, moving his main residence to Prague Castle. Vratislav then built a second church in Prague Castle dedicated to St George.

3. GROWING UP OF THE YOUNG PRINCE WENCESLAS

At the time when Vratislav took the dukedom, a major ritual took place celebrating the first cutting of hair of the growing Prince Wenceslas. Special celebration of the cutting of the hair was originally a pagan ritual, known in the east as well as in the west and adapted by the church. It was a custom in such a ritual for the person who was cutting the hair to become a kind of godfather to the child. This ritual took place at various ages, once at a very early age and once at the age when the child was passed from the exclusive care of the mother to supervision by the father. Russians had their hair cut at the age of 2 or 3, while in Poland it was at the age of 7, and Serbs had their ritual at the age of 1, 3, 8, 12, or even at 15 years old.

From all the information available it can be estimated that Wenceslas was about 7 years old at the ceremonial cutting of his hair. According to legend, Vratislav called a bishop with all his accompanying priests and the ceremony took place in the Church of St Mary in Prague Castle, as St George's Church was not yet built. Once the bishop with his priests finished singing their liturgy, the bishop then stood Wenceslas on the steps of the altar and blessed him so, "Our Lord Jesus Christ, bless this child with the blessings you have bestowed on all fair and just people." After the blessing, other dukes cut Wenceslas's hair.

After this ceremony Wenceslas started to learn all that it was necessary for him to know. Ludmila, his grandmother, had a great influence on him. Besides being with his parents in Prague Castle, then their main residence, he also spent time with his grandmother in Melnik and Tetin. It was Ludmila who saw to it that Wenceslas was taught how to read and write in the Slavonic language first, most probably by her Slavonic priest Paul, himself a pupil of Cyril (Constantine) and Methodius. From Paul, he would also have learnt about the Graeco-Slavonic liturgy translated for the local people and approved by the Pope. He would have learnt about Byzantine Empire, other Slavonic nations, their Germanic neighbours in the west and about Rome, the seat of the Pope. Ludmila would also have told him about Svatopluk of Moravia and how he expelled pupils of Cyril and Methodius. (See fig. 3.1.)

Wenceslas also learned how to produce wine and helped with the harvesting of corn. He learned how to bake bread for religious purposes and this was one of his favourite tasks well into adulthood. (See fig. 3.2.)

In his boyhood, he was sent to Budec by his father Vratislav. Budec was a religious and educational establishment and a castle. Wenceslas was to be educated there in the reading and writing of Latin, then the religious language of priests coming from the west and also a very important diplomatic language. The two religious services, one in Latin from the west, and the Graeco-Slavonic in the Old Slavonic language from the east, lived alongside each other for some time. As there were no new priests trained in the Graeco-Slavonic liturgy, this gradually gave way to the Latin version.

There is no mention that Wenceslas would have learned German, the language of the neighbouring areas. One of the legends does suggest that he learnt Greek. There was the link with the Greek missionaries Cyril and Methodius and the Moravian priests educated by them and thus most probably Ludmila's priest Paul would have known some Greek and would have taught Wenceslas what he knew. After all the Slavonic writing Hlaholice was derived from Greek and this would have been of interest to any teacher of Hlaholice. However, some historians argue that at the time of Wenceslas's boyhood, there was no documented need for the Greek language in Bohemia and that the comment may have been just added during copying and rewriting of the legend in a Russian monastery, as it was in Russia that the knowledge of Greek was highly respected.

All the legends agree that Wenceslas was a gifted pupil and soon could read religious books in Latin as well as any good bishop or priest. His teacher in Budec was a priest called Uceno, who may have been of Czech origin, but had obviously studied abroad.

In Budec Wenceslas also took part in games with his fellow pupils, and was prepared for various duties as would be expected of a prince and future heir to the throne. So he trained in horse-riding, the throwing of a lance, swordsmanship and other battle skills.

His grandmother Ludmila, a devout Christian herself, taught him the importance of true faith in God and Christianity. She herself arranged for money and clothes to be given to poor people, without them knowing where it came from. The happy childhood of Wenceslas was shattered when his father Vratislav suddenly died. It is not known how he died, but it is assumed by historians that his death occurred in a battle defending the country against Magyars.

Wenceslas was only 13 years old at that time. He, as the oldest male, was expected to step on to the throne. The ceremony was performed in Prague Castle in front of Saint George's Church, which had been built by Vratislav. When the people had assembled, young Wenceslas was seated on the duke's stone throne, the very throne which had stood there for as long as people could remember. At this ceremony he was reminded of his forefather Premysl's humble origins, and was shown Premysl's sandals and the bag made from wood bast. (This tradition of showing Premysl's sandals and bag during the enthronement of ruling dukes and kings was carried out until the year 1228.) The legends say that from the moment Wenceslas was put on the duke's throne his brother Boleslav, who was a few years younger as it is believed, was subordinated to him.

As Wenceslas was only 13 years old, it was decided by the elders that his mother Drahomira was to rule on his behalf. However, she was not given full powers and she was obliged to confer and to take advice from her mother-in-law, Ludmila. Ludmila was also entrusted by the elders with overseeing the education and upbringing of the two princes, Wenceslas and Boleslav.

Drahomira resented taking advice from Ludmila and the fact that Ludmila was entrusted with overseeing her two sons' upbringing. Drahomira did not come from the Czech tribe but from another far distant Slavonic tribe, which was still pagan at that time. Although while her husband was alive, she had conformed to his Christian way of life, once he was dead she returned to paganism and started to surround herself with her own people who would support the pagan way of life.

Ludmila was aware of Drahomira's resentment of her and suggested she should leave Prague Castle for Tetin, a castle with estates, which was hers to live in in retirement. But that was not enough. Drahomira sent two assassins, Tunna and Gommon with a military escort to Tetin. After they overcame her guard, they strangled Ludmila with her own veil on Saturday 16 September 921, while she was praying. However some legends suggest that rope was used and not her veil. One legend also tells us that she pleaded with her killers to be killed with the sword as some early Christian martyrs had died, spilling their blood for Jesus Christ. She was denied her last wish.

Drahomira further stepped up the suppression of Christianity by confiscating the property of many priests and exiling them. There was pressure on Wenceslas, as their young duke, to abandon his Christian ways and beliefs and to join in pagan ceremonies and feasts. However, Wenceslas stayed faithful to Christianity and very often prayed at night, secretly inviting those Christian priests left in the country to join him. Some of the legends talk about Wenceslas's dream, a vision, in which he saw the death of his grandmother Ludmila and the suppression of Christianity by his mother Drahomira.

Tunna and Gommon were well rewarded for their act by gifts of gold, silver and estates from Drahomira and were given administrative powers to rule the country with Drahomira. But their good fortune did not last. They fell out with Drahomira and she started to plan their downfall. When Tunna heard of it, he escaped abroad with all his relatives, never to return. Gommon was not so lucky, and was caught with his brother as they tried to escape. They were sentenced to death. Drahomira also had all their relatives, old and young, destroyed in one day.

Ludmila was buried in Tetin and people came to her grave and prayed there. She had been known for her pious life and soon people reported miracles happening near her grave. Drahomira had a small wooden church built over the grave, and dedicated to St Michael, so that any miracles or special heavenly signs happening there could be attributed to St Michael and not to the blessed Ludmila. (See fig. 3.3.)

During the rule of Drahomira, in 922, Arnulf, Duke of Bavaria, invaded Bohemia with his army. The Czech army, with the young Duke Wenceslas in front, then about 15 years old, went to meet them in the border region. There are no detailed reports about the purpose or the outcome of this military encounter. There is no evidence of a change in relationship between Bohemia and Bavaria, or indeed Saxony, as it was not so long before that in 921, King Henry the Fowler of Saxony with his big army had set siege to Regensburg. He had forced Arnulf to accept his rule and open the gates to him without a fight.

In the east of Bohemia, there was another dukedom, the duke of which was married to Arnulf's sister, his name is not known. But we know the son's name was Slavnik and from that they are called Slavniks by historians. As Arnulf's daughter Judith married Henry the Fowler of Saxony, the Slavniks were also related to this important family. It was during the rule of Drahomira, a very unsettled time, that they may have wanted to gain influence over the Premyslid dukedom and asked Arnulf to invade.

4. MANHOOD - RULING AND LIVING UP TO HIS CHRISTIAN BELIEFS

In around 925, Wenceslas, at the age of 18 years, took power and started to rule on his own. Christianity had survived in peoples' hopes and memories of the generosity of his grandmother Ludmila. He assembled all the noblemen in Prague Castle and spoke to them, clearly outlining his future policy. (See fig. 4.) He told them that never again must anybody be denied the freedom to learn about Jesus Christ and to live according to his teaching.

But his firm stand polarised the two camps, one which supported him and the other which supported his mother Drahomira. Blood was spilled, and Wenceslas called the noblemen again and once more stressed that he would rule according to Christian principles but at the same time he would uphold the most punishing laws of the land. He warned them that they must no longer stain their hands with murder as he would not hesitate to execute them.

On the advice of his elders, who were warning that his mother might want to murder both him and his brother as she had murdered Ludmila, he expelled his mother, a source of unrest, from Prague Castle to Budec.

During this early period young Wenceslas performed another heroic act when he put the lives of his soldiers and those of the enemy soldiers before his own life. Several legends refer to this event although they do not date it exactly.

Another neighbouring duke, Radslav of Kourim tried to extend his rule over Wenceslas's dukedom. He started to provoke Wenceslas by unfriendly actions. Wenceslas tried to mediate but it led to nothing and soon the two armies of both dukedoms were marching against each other. Wenceslas wanted once more to stop the unnecessary bloodshed of soldiers on both sides of the conflict. He asked Radslav to meet him in a man to man duel. Under the established rules of such a duel, after the death of one of the dukes, the other would take over everything in the other dukedom including the country and the people.

I was told that they met near another settlement which found itself near the village of Pristopim near the town of Cesky Broad. There are no detailed reports about the encounter. It is suggested that Radslav chose heavy armoury, sword and lance, while Wenceslas kept his helmet and iron shirt and chose a light sword. Radslav threw his lance at Wenceslas but missed.

The legend says that Radslav saw a picture of the Holy Cross on Wenceslas's forehead and at once realised that if God was on his enemy's side that he would not be able to overcome the man. He threw his sword aside and knelt before Wenceslas. Under the traditional pagan rules of such a duel, it was up to Wenceslas to finish him off, to kill him. However, Wenceslas spared Radslav's life. He lifted Radslav up from his knees and kissed him to seal the peace between them. Although Wenceslas took the Kourim dukedom, he let Radslav administer it for him till the end of Radslav's life.

A helmet, reported to have belonged to Wenceslas and kept in St Vitus Cathedral, does have a cross which extends over the forehead and could very well have reflected in the sun during the battle. (See fig. 4.2.3.)

Duke Wenceslas very much believed in Christianity and saw the true benefits of living the Christian way of life as opposed to paganism. He invited priests and their pupils back from exile and with great celebrations they re-opened churches. Where priests had been sold into slavery, he bought them out. He welcomed priests from abroad to his dukedom. Very often, they were the source of new books for him. The legends tell us that he provided them with shelter, clothes and money for them to preach and to spread Christianity.

In those days, individual nobleman built churches in their castles and settlements and it was they who hired priests for their churches. The priests were not appointed by the nearest bishop or any other religious organisation. Thus the priests had to depend on the generosity of the employing noblemen. It was only natural for Wenceslas to lead the way in supporting priests and monks who came to the country.

It was later, once the unrest settled down, that because of his Christian beliefs, he questioned his decision to expel his mother, and he asked her to return. Drahomira was not given any of her powers back on her return to Prague Castle and she accepted the way her son Wenceslas ruled.

As one of the first acts of his rule, Wenceslas brought the body of his grandmother Ludmila from Tetin on Friday 21 October 925. Much loved by him and by the people, Ludmila was buried at Prague Castle, in St George's Church. She was interred with all honours by her Slavonic priest Paul. People remembered Ludmila's kindness, Christian ways and her martyrdom, and they frequently visited her grave and prayed to her. The translation of her body to St George's Church and the placing of her body under or in the altar was accepted in those days of early Christianity as canonisation and the recognition of sainthood. The recognition and respect of her as a saint grew with time. Her name changed slightly over the years and is written in modern Czech as Ludmila, while in her day it was Lidmila, both meaning 'loved by people'.

Wenceslas started to re-establish the Christian way of life in his country. He built many churches and most would have been built of wood, an easily available building material at that time, but as such we have no remains of them and there are no specific records.

One church we know about was in Prague Castle and built of stone. The church was supposed to be dedicated at first to St Emmeram, a Bavarian saint. Each mission had its saint, whose relics they would give to the newly created churches. Thus the Graeco-Slavonic mission created several churches dedicated to St Clement, Franks' missions were establishing churches dedicated to St Martin and Saxony had their St Vitus. The bringing of St Vitus's relics to Saxony is associated with their freedom and success over the Franks. It is also associated with the succession of their ruling dynasty to the king's and ultimately the Holy Roman Imperial throne. Henry the Fowler donated an arm of St Vitus to Wenceslas. It is not certian if this was before or after the work on the church had started.

One legend in Bohemia says that Wenceslas called all the best craftsmen from abroad to build this church in stone. Building with stone and mortar was not widely known in Bohemia at that time. Today, only parts of the foundations are left underneath the Gothic St Vitus Cathedral. From the foundations and from knowledge of similar constructions elsewhere, Josef Cibulka outlined how this church could have looked. Such a building would have helped with the request for a separate bishopric for Bohemia and this may have been the purpose of Wenceslas's intended journey to Rome.

Fig. 4.1 St Vitus Rotunda, a sophisticated construction for its time, in Prague Castle. Drawing by Josef Cibulka

Wenceslas had priests amongst his advisors, and lived and ruled like a Christian king. (See fig. 4.2.) Like his grandmother Ludmila, he gave money and clothes to the poor. He built orphanages for children displaced by previous wars.

In the depths of winter he helped local people in need who did not have others to look after them. With his faithful page Podevin, he delivered wood, food and money to those who needed it.

This is recorded in a later legend, 'Ut annuntietur', written at the end of the 13th or beginning of the 14th century, where it is said that Wenceslas had the custom of delivering wood to widows and orphans in winter, at night and secretly. Wenceslas did not want anybody to see him doing this good deed and so he went at night to his own forest to collect the wood. A gamekeeper noticed that somebody was stealing the wood, and tried to catch the culprit, but failed. So he reported it to Wenceslas and was only told that he had to try even harder to catch the thief, and when he did so, he should properly whip him, but he should not take the wood away from him and he should let him go. The gamekeeper was a little puzzled by this order but as it was from his duke he did not question it.

Indeed the next night he caught the thief and, not recognising his master, he pushed him to the ground and beat him. He then let him go off with the wood. Apparently this happened several times. According to the same legend, his page Podevin did not feel any cold when following Wenceslas in his footsteps on these missions of mercy. The winters in Bohemia are about 10 degrees colder than in England and snow can stay for months, and as proper shoes were scarce in those days, long walks in snow should merit our admiration.

This story about Wenceslas, written three or four centuries after his death, at a time when he was already canonised as a saint may have been influenced by pious admiration for the sainthood, and some historians suggest that the story of beating by the game-keeper may have been added at a later date. However Wenceslas's help for the needy in principle is recognised as true, and so on the painting in Stara Boleslav he is simply shown with Podevin, carrying wood to a widow with children. (See fig. 4.3.)

Also the same symbol of Wenceslas carrying wood is shown on one of the main gates to the St Vitus Cathedral in Prague Castle and another such picture can be seen in the St Wenceslas Chapel.

Slavery was still flourishing in those days in Europe. People were forced to become slaves because of indebtedness, and children because of the poverty of their parents.

Some slaves from Central Europe found their way as far as Arabia. I remember meeting students from Egypt in Norwich in 1993, who told me they knew of Egyptians with blond hair, who without doubt would have been descendants of people from Europe displaced by the mediaeval slave trade.

When there was a need for young men to serve as altar boys in the churches, Wenceslas would go to the market and select them from slaves, whom he then bought. In one of the legends, Kristian says that Wenceslas would buy slaves and have them christened and set them free. Wenceslas freed people from the burden of slavery whenever he could.

Prague was an important centre of the international slave trade in the 10th century as documented by the international trader and writer, Ibrahim ibn Jacob. We cannot however expect to see Wenceslas's actions as trying to abolish slavery, but just to help those most in need, as a result of his Christian principles.

He also reformed the penal system. It was a time when rough morals and rough justice very often still prevailed. Wenceslas had gallows and places of physical punishment torn down where there were no proper judges appointed by him. He also tried to reduce the number of capital punishments, as this practice conflicted with his Christian beliefs and with the Ten Commandments.

Wenceslas very often sat in on trials ensuring that they were fair. However, when the judges agreed on a sentence of death, he preferred to leave rather than be present at the sentencing, according to the legends.

Wenceslas also visited prisoners and educated them in a Christian way of life so that after genuine repentance of their sins, they could be released back into society.

But Wenceslas maintained order. He in person checked on soldiers on guard-duty; if they were found drunk they were punished by flogging. The same punishment was used for people who avoided work.

As the duke of his country he had to maintain castles at the gateways in the border regions. All legends credit him with giving the best arms and clothing to his soldiers.

There is no doubt about his personal bravery, that he fought alongside his soldiers when it was needed. His skull, which is kept in St Vitus Cathedral, shows a wound which was fully healed before his death. But there is no mention of what must have been an injury from a battle in the surviving legends.

5. WENCESLAS'S OWN WAY OF LIFE

As Wenceslas wanted his people to be freed from barbarian and pagan practices, he himself lived very modestly. He avoided banquets and overindulgence in food. Indeed, one of the paintings in the basilica in Stara Boleslav depicts him dispersing a pagan gathering of festivities and sacrifices to pagan gods. That is reported to have happened near Tursko.

One legend says that if he indulged in eating and drinking, the next day he went to the church and begged the priests for forgiveness as he had sinned the night before.

I have already reported that he was well educated and indeed he frequently carried a book under his coat, so he could read it in his spare moments. One of his books, which he had with him when he died in Stara Boleslav is reported to be kept to this day in Rome.

All the legends agree that Wenceslas was deeply religious. For example it is said in the Kristian's Legend that Duke Wenceslas went barefoot in winter from castle to castle, visiting churches many times, leaving traces of blood in his footsteps on icy paths. According to the same legend, he dressed in a simple shirt made from horsehair, then covered by woollen cloth, as monks would wear, and on top he wore a beautiful royal robe so that he shone in the eyes of God and his people alike.

One legend tells us that Wenceslas was a virgin when he died, while another indicates that he was married and had a son called Zbraslav. However, history does not tell us much about this part of his life, just a few small fragments have been found. According to one fragment he was forced to marry very young and his marriage was an unhappy one. According to another fragment, his wife was unfaithful to him and he allowed her to marry the man she had had the relationship with. These fragments of information must be understood in the context of society over 1000 years ago. It was almost 50 years later, in 982, that the second bishop of Prague, St Adalbert, undertook as one of his main objectives to introduce Christian morals in Bohemia, where having several wives had been an accepted way of life since pagan days.

Whatever his personal life may have been, it did not detract from any of his good deeds, as they were reported in the legends and by the people from generation to generation.

6. NEED FOR PEACE

But there were other difficult times for Wenceslas, when King Henry the Fowler of Saxony and Duke Arnulf of Bavaria marched into his country in 929 with a huge army. Rather than fighting a losing battle, he chose to follow his predecessors and pay dues for the alliance annually in silver and cattle. Cosmas reports that it was 120 oxen and 500 hrivnas (weights) of silver. This specific information is disputed by some modern historians, as being confused with payments in later years and concluding that it is not known what were the payments during Wenceslas's rule.

The agreement gave Wenceslas the necessary peace and stability he needed for his country. It was not long before that Moravia, a Slavonic state to the south east of Bohemia, had been destroyed. It was only a year before that his grandfather's dukedom Stodor (on his mother's side), north of Bohemia, was destroyed by Saxony for defying the acceptance of Christianity and subordination. Wenceslas may have provided military to help the Stodor people in their defence and may even have fought and received his injury there. The invasion in 929 by Saxony could have been in punishment of Wenceslas's and the Bohemian intervention.

Agreed payments may be understood as alliance payments but also as payments to stop further raids. Such payments were customary in those days and were also paid by Saxony to the newly settled Magyar horsemen to stop their raids into Bavaria and Saxony. Bohemia benefited from this agreement too. Wenceslas had a good relationship with the bishop of Regensburg in Bavaria who administered Bohemia on religious grounds and there were a number of German priests in Bohemia who were welcomed in the country.

Peace with King Henry the Fowler meant for Wenceslas that he was on friendly terms with him. That is when it is believed he was given the arm of St Vitus and thus his church was dedicated to St Vitus and not to St Emmeram. A later legend also says that Wenceslas was given the title of King.

One legend from the 13th century called 'Oriente iam sole' tells an interesting story about Wenceslas and Henry the Fowler. Wenceslas was taking part in Saxony's assembly, which most probably took place in today's Aachen, and was chaired by Henry the Fowler himself. All the dukes were already assembled, but Wenceslas was late. On the way, he had received mass in a church and was thus delayed. Henry felt insulted by Wenceslas's lateness and ordered the dukes present (under threat of beheading), to ignore Wenceslas when he arrived and to refuse him a place. Finally Wenceslas entered. To the amazement of the assembled dukes, Henry the Fowler suddenly stood up, greeted Wenceslas himself, and sat Wenceslas next to him, beside his throne. Henry then explained to the assembled dukes that he saw an angel accompanying Wenceslas and in the heavenly light he saw the sign of a cross on Wenceslas's forehead. (See fig. 6.1.)

The good relationship between Wenceslas and King Henry provided the inspiration for other paintings in St Wenceslas's Chapel in Prague Castle and some historians conclude that Wenceslas saw in King Henry the Fowler, the successor of Charles the Great, the Holy Roman Emperor and defender of the Christian faith.

Wenceslas carried on with the construction of St Vitus Church and was even contemplating going to Rome to dedicate himself to the religious life. He wanted to finish his church, which no doubt would have helped his application to the Pope for a bishopric in Prague. There was some kind of discontent in the country however, and he wanted to deal with it. One legend says that he discussed with his brother Boleslav the possibility of passing the rule of the country over to Boleslav once he went to Rome.

7. PRESSURE FROM HIS BROTHER BOLESLAV AND OTHERS

His younger brother Boleslav, who administered the eastern part of the country, east of the river Elbe, surrounded himself with critics of Wenceslas's rule, indeed, the same men who were in power under Drahomira's rule. Some noblemen did not like the fact that Wenceslas tried to implement his Christian beliefs, helping poor and enslaved people and living modestly himself. Wenceslas also gave generous support to the church.

Pagan customs and ethics were still in place and the whole society could be better described as half pagan and half Christian. Thus for the rebellious noblemen, the deposing of Wenceslas could have meant going back to the old days and customs.

Besides the potential religious reasons there may have been also another. Payments to King Henry the Fowler of Saxony must have been collected from the whole country and could have been another reason for the rebellious noblemen to want to depose Wenceslas and install Boleslav. As we now know, the war Boleslav led afterwards with King Henry's successor, King Otto I, was about subordination and payments of annual peace contributions, called *tribut pacis* in Latin.

Some historians argue that from the religious point of view, Boleslav was also introduced to Christianity by his grandmother Ludmila and her priest Paul. Boleslav also had a church in his castle and employed a priest. Therefore it could be argued that it must have been the rebellious noblemen who persuaded Boleslav to take part in Wenceslas's murder, not the other way round. According to the First Slavonic Legend, which was written at the time of Boleslav's rule, the noblemen surrounding him told Boleslav that it was actually Wenceslas who wanted to kill him.

Boleslav was very ambitious, as can be seen from his years of rule. Thus it is a good question how much persuasion he needed to agree to take part in the murder of his own brother in his own castle. We can only speculate about the possible reasons behind the murder but it can be blamed on the struggle for power, as has happened many times before and many times after throughout history.

8. WENCESLAS'S DEATH

Boleslav invited Wenceslas to his castle on the river Elbe in today's Stara Boleslav for the celebration feast of Saints Cosmas and Damian, then falling on Sunday 27 September. Their church was in the grounds of Boleslav's castle. Duke Wenceslas customarily visited churches on their feast days throughout his country and even abroad, so he did not find Boleslav's invitation at all suspicious.

The feast celebrations may have also been linked with the Christening of Boleslav's newly born son. Some sources mention this and indeed the name given to the baby, Strachkvas, meaning when translated from Czech something like 'Terrifying Drink' or 'Drink of Horror', reflected the tragic event.

Wenceslas had not intended to stay overnight with his company and he wanted to leave after the religious ceremony. However, he was persuaded by his brother to stay overnight. So in the afternoon they all saddled horses and both Wenceslas's and Boleslav's knights joined in games in the court of Boleslav's castle.

During the main evening meal, a servant tried to warn Wenceslas, telling him that Boleslav was planning to kill him and that he should not hesitate, take his horse and leave. Wenceslas did not. One of the legends says that during the evening dinner, the assassins three times stood up, hiding their daggers, ready to attack but there were always enough of Wenceslas's knights around to make the assassins sit down again. Wenceslas raised his glass of wine to toast St Michael, who accompanies souls to heaven, just to let them know that he was not afraid.

Once dinner was over, Wenceslas would have prayed in his room long into the night as he had done many times before. I would assume his knights would have taken turns to stand guard.

But Boleslav did not go to bed and pray, he and his accomplices had to make a new plan. They met in the Court of Hnevsa in the castle grounds. They knew that Wenceslas went to church very early every morning to pray before other people arrived for the service. Just to ensure that nobody upset their plan, they ordered their people to ring the church bell earlier than normal. They also ordered the church door to be kept locked.

Early in the morning, when the church bell rang, Wenceslas, ahead of his knights, hastened to church for his morning prayers, relieved that nothing had happened during the night.

Outside the building he met his brother Boleslav and thanked him for the hospitality given him the night before. Boleslav replied that he had even better hospitality ready for him now. He drew his sword against the unarmed Wenceslas. Wenceslas was astonished by his brother's attack. He was trained and experienced in combat, but all he could do was to swerve so that Boleslav's first blow to Wenceslas's head missed and only cut Wenceslas's ear. Wenceslas said in disbelief, "What do you think you are doing, brother?" Wenceslas attacked Boleslav and pushed him to the ground. Another conspirator, named Tuza, ran to the scene and swang his sword against Wenceslas and cut his hand.

Wenceslas's hand injury forced him to let Boleslav go and run towards the door of Saints Cosmas and Damian Church instead. It was locked. Two other conspirators, Tira and

Cesta, caught up with him at the door, and killed Wenceslas with their lances piercing him through his back. Hnevsa joined in and thrust his sword through Wenceslas's side. According to the First Slavonic Legend, Wenceslas died immediately. Some legends say that Good King Wenceslas forgave his brother even as he lay dying.

But legends vary. They all agree that Boleslav was not successful in his first attempt to kill Wenceslas and it was Wenceslas who pushed Boleslav to the ground. Dean Fiser, from St Wenceslas's basilica told me that according to the version of events passed on from generation to generation in Stara Boleslav, under pagan rules of combat, it was up to Wenceslas to kill his brother Boleslav, once he pushed him to the ground and wrestled his sword out of Boleslav's hand. But Wenceslas's Christian beliefs were too strong. He asked God to forgive his brother for what he had tried to do, then spared Boleslav's life.

This however gave a chance to Boleslav, instead of thanking his brother Wenceslas for sparing his life, to shout for the help of his accomplices. They emerged on the scene, at which they had been until then just bystanders, drawing their swords and lances ready to attack. Wenceslas realising that he was outnumbered five to one, decided to make a run for the church, as in those days a church was already recognised as a sanctuary where nobody's life could be taken or harmed. However, on reaching the door, he found it locked. The assassins closed in, the first lance went through his body from the back as he desperately tried to open the door. Some historical sources indicate that further blows followed and his body was quartered. One other of Wenceslas's men, called Mstina, was also murdered at the scene. (See figs 8.1, 8.2.)

Afterwards Boleslav sent his soldiers to Wenceslas's castle in Prague and another massacre followed of Wenceslas's supporters, including their small children. If Wenceslas had a small son called Zbraslav, then he would have died too. The young children, according to Kristian's Legend, were drowned in the depths of the river Vltava. Many of the women were given to other men for wives. Priests and monks were persecuted and expelled.

The First Slavonic Legend also includes a suggestion made by Tira to Boleslav that they should kill his mother too. Boleslav replied that as she had no escape that they could deal with the others first. They left Wenceslas's body dismembered and unburied.

It was the priest, Krastej, who laid Wenceslas's body in front of the church and covered it with a sheet. When his mother heard Wenceslas had been killed, she went to look for his body and on finding it, she bent over it in tears. Then she gathered all his limbs and took his body to the priest's room, washed and dressed her dead son. She laid his body in the middle of the church. Drahomira then left, hurrying abroad, as her own life was in danger, never to return. When Boleslav returned he found her gone. Boleslav called priest Paul to pray over the body of Wenceslas and it was buried next to the church in the grounds of Boleslav's castle, later known as Stara Boleslav.

The spilled blood of Wenceslas would not seep into the ground for three days and on the third day it showed up on the church wall. Everybody was puzzled by it. The writer of the Legend expresses his hope that God will, with pleas from Wenceslas now in heaven, show even greater miracles.

Wenceslas's sister, Pribyslava when she heard about the tragedy, rushed to Boleslav's castle. She had a dream that an ear cut off from Wenceslas was lying at the scene of the tragedy unburied. She indeed found it and put it with the rest of Wenceslas's body.

The murder shocked the Czech people and the news of it travelled across the whole of Europe. It was reported in many historical documents of that time and legends were written by priests and monks. Good King Wenceslas and his kind and caring rule was not forgotten by his people and priests. They prayed to him, and respect for him as a martyr grew immediately.

The year of his death is now listed as 935 by most of the modern historians but it was listed as 929 not so long ago. It is interesting thing that the day of his death, 28 September, falls on a Monday in both years. The First Slavonic Legend says it was 929, while there were other years like 928, 936, 938 and 939 listed throughout the centuries. More recent studies indicate that the most likely year of Wenceslas's death is the year 935. This fits with other available facts. A study was also made in 1972 by F.V. Mares, which showed that the year 929 was an error made in the First Slavonic Legend when the year 935 was transcribed from Hlaholice to Cyrillic.

9. TIMES AFTER WENCESLAS

Boleslav moved his residence and the centre of his rule to Prague Castle. For some time the situation in Bohemia was unsettled as Boleslav, with sword and soldiers, secured allegiance from Wenceslas's supporters.

Podevin escaped the massacre and stayed abroad in Germany for some time but returned a year later when the situation had quietened down. He hid at home and in other places, but one day he felt a great pain in his heart, the pain he had felt after losing his master Wenceslas. He took his sword and went to a court and house in Boleslav's castle where he knew the leader of the conspiracy lived, which had led to the assassination of Good King Wenceslas. He found him in his steam bath, as reported in Kristian's Legend. No name is mentioned but from the First Slavonic Legend we know that the night before the conspirators met at Hnevsa's Court.

This conspirator, not knowing who was at the door, welcomed Podevin with the typical Czech greeting 'be healthy, my friend, be healthy'. Podevin with his heart full of pain, replied to him, according to Kristian's Legend, 'God will care for my health and salvation, but you have lost all your health and salvation long ago and you will die in sin for ever.' Podevin could not hold his anger any more, and killed the assassin to avenge his master's death. He then escaped from the castle to a nearby forest.

When Boleslav heard about this, he had the forest encircled by soldiers and they caught Podevin. He was hanged outside Boleslav's castle on the edge of the forest. His body was left hanging there for two or three years and was then buried on the same spot. It is said his body was untouched by birds and animals for all that time. The hair, beard and nails grew long and the hair turned white, as if Podevin had continued to live and age. Also reported were sightings of a heavenly light seen later over the grave. People started to bring sacrifices to the grave where they prayed to God and Podevin. The author of one legend, a monk who signed his work as 'Kristian', notes that he was reluctant to write about this miracle which seemed so great, but he met so many people who witnessed it that he could not leave it out of his legend. Today on that spot stands a small chapel dedicated to the blessed Podevin.

In the First Slavonic Legend, which was written by a priest or priests who went east to Bulgaria and Russia, it is said that Boleslav repented his great sin and praying to God, he admitted it, saying, "I sinned and I am aware of my sin." Although Wenceslas was first buried in Boleslav's castle in Stara Boleslav, Boleslav had his body transferred from there to Prague Castle almost three years after his death on 4 March 938 (or 932 if we assume his death occurred in 929). Again the date falls on the same day of the week, Sunday, in both years.

On the orders of Boleslav, the transfer had to take place at night. Good King Wenceslas was reburied in the rotunda of St Vitus. The body of his page Podevin was also transferred from Stara Boleslav at some later date and was buried on the outside of the rotunda in the cemetery, so that only the wall separated him from his master, Wenceslas. In those days the transference of Wenceslas's body to the church and its being placed near the altar was accepted as canonisation by the then Roman Catholic Church.

On the political front, King Henry the Fowler of Saxony suffered a stroke in the autumn of 935 and died in 936 and thus could not interfere in Bohemia after Wenceslas's death. His son Otto I, now in power, entered into a fourteen-year war against Boleslav until Boleslav surrendered to him in 950 and agreed to pay dues for peace and alliance. One source indicates that it was Boleslav II, his son, who agreed the peace, because he and Otto I had married sisters, the daughters of the Anglo-Saxon King, Edward the Elder.

Boleslav was married to a German princess, called Biagota and they had four children: daughters Doubrava (also Doubravka) and Mlada and sons Strachkvas and Boleslav II, who later succeeded him in running the country.

In 955, Boleslav helped Otto I to defeat Magyars in a battle on the river Lech. It may have been one of the most important battles in 10th century Europe, because the Magyars were defeated and were incapable of further raids on other parts of Europe. They settled for an agricultural life and a new independent Hungarian kingdom was born. One part of Boleslav's army fought a victorious battle with Magyars in Moravia and it is believed that after that Boleslav had Moravia under his rule, as well as ruling tribes in Upper Selesia and as far as Krakow in today's Poland.

Boleslav's daughter Doubravka married the first recorded ruler of Poland, Mieszko I (also Mieczislav) in 965. With Doubravka went priests and thus Christianity spread further east. Mieszko's main castle was in Gniezno.

The younger daughter Mlada was sent by her father Boleslav to Rome to plead for independent religious administration in Prague. But Boleslav did not achieve this during his lifetime. He died in 972. It was very soon afterwards that his son Boleslav II, who became the ruling duke, achieved the establishment of the bishopric of Prague. This is hailed as one of his most important diplomatic achievements. One must add that it was also due to the kind understanding of the bishop of Regensburg, Wolfgang, later known as Saint Wolfgang who administered Bohemia. He agreed to the Prague bishopric while others were advising against it.

The Prague bishopric was established in 973 and with that there was also permission to establish the first convent. Boleslav II, who was also called 'Religious', invited the order of Benedictine monks into the country and established the first convent in Prague Castle alongside St George's Church. His sister Mlada was the first abbess. She died in 994. Her brother Strachkvas dedicated his life to priesthood and spent a considerable time in Regensburg in Bavaria.

Boleslav II married an Anglo-Saxon Princess, Adivea (Elfgifa), a sister of Otto I's wife - Edgith. Princess Adivea came with her sister to the Continent when they were very young, about 13 or 14 years old or even younger. They were daughters of King Edward the Elder.

Engagements and marriages between children were nothing unusual in those days and one author suggests that Good King Wenceslas brought Adivea to Bohemia for his nephew Boleslav II as a result of his meeting with King Henry the Fowler after her sister Edgith's wedding to his son Otto I. Adivea brought to Bohemia a positive influence in the form of an Anglo-Saxon mint, which was recognised as the most advanced at the time.

It is believed that once on the Continent, Adivea (Elfgifa) accepted the name Emma, which was the Norman equivalent of her Anglo-Saxon name. She had her own coins struck in her own mint in Melnik with her name and title 'Emma Regina', indicating that she was from a royal family. Her coins were made by her own Anglo-Saxon mint-masters and were better than those of her husband Boleslav II. Her name is also associated with the illustration of the Wolfentbuttel manuscript which contains Gumpold's legend of Saint Wenceslas.

The first bishop of Prague was Deitmar, a Saxon priest who spent a long time in Bohemia and who could speak Czech. He died in 982 and the second bishop was Vojtech, who was elected on 19 January 982 in Levy Hradec, an important castle, known to have the first Christian church built in Bohemia. Vojtech was of princely origin from the Slavnik tribe. Some historians argue that having a Slavnik for a bishop in Prague, serving the Premyslids, as it was perceived in those days, indicated that all the Slavniks were under the rule of Premyslids.

Vojtech, less than thirty years old and eager, threw himself wholeheartedly into pastoral work, converting a still half pagan society. He was an intellectual and helped to spread respect for St Wenceslas. The oldest song dedicated to St Wenceslas is believed to be his work. He also founded a new Benedictine Abbey, Brevnov, in Prague.

However he was very critical of his own work and achievements in converting this half pagan society, in which various pagan practices, including the taking of several wives, were still acceptable. Priests were marrying at that time and they too were under his critical eye. The slave trade with Christians was also attacked by Bishop Vojtech, and he bought slaves out of slavery whenever he could, using church money. He also gave money to the poor. This brought him into conflict with some of the priests, who complained to Boleslav II. Final conflict came when Vojtech gave sanctuary in St George's Convent in Prague Castle in 994 to a repentant adulterous noblewoman. The family feud resulted in violation of the sanctuary. The accused woman was dragged out and killed. Vojtech had to act to denounce such a great violation with equally drastic measures by pronouncing a curse on the guilty clan (believed by some to be Vrsovci) and excommunicating them.

The whole matter created an uneasy situation, and Vojtech, unhappy about his position, left Bohemia for Rome for the second time in 995, spending some time in Hungary on his way.

It may have been Vojtech's departure from Prague that made Duke Boleslav II realise the threat that Slavniks posed to him. They were related to Otto III's imperial family and were on friendly terms with the Polish ruler, Boleslav Chrabry (The Bold). They were economically strong as they minted their own coins and even had their own army.

At that time, both the Premyslids and Slavniks contributed one regiment of soldiers to Otto III's expedition against the pagan Bodrci tribe in the north.

Slavniks are recognised as the eastern wing of the Zlicane tribe, whose Duke Radslav of Kourim had submitted to Duke Wenceslas in the previously described duel. But time had passed and Slavnik's many sons: Sobebor, Spytimir, Pobraslav, Porej and Caslav, did not feel loyalty to Boleslav II. Thus, as most Slavnik soldiers were in the north and the castles were barely defended by token soldiers, the Premyslids decided to attack their main seat in Libice.

The surprise attack, believed to have been led by the Vrsovci clan, took place on 28 September 995, fifty years from the date of St Wenceslas's death. As the defenders of Libice tried to buy time and agree a ceasefire, claiming that they wanted to celebrate the feast of St Wenceslas, Boleslav's soldiers shouted back from below the castle walls, "If your saint is Wenceslas, ours is Boleslav." Thus wrote monk Bruno in his legend about St Vojtech. The siege of Libice lasted two days, resulting in the total destruction of the castle and the killing of all the remaining Slavnik men, women and children. Other Slavnik castles followed suit.

Vojtech never returned to Bohemia. He acted as advisor to Otto III. Later he went to spread Christianity to pagan Prussia and was killed near Koningsberg as a suspected Polish spy. The ruler of Poland, Boleslav Chrabry, the son of Doubravka and Mieszko, paid Vojtech's weight in gold for the body to be brought to Gniezno.

Vojtech was recognised as a saint and is known as Saint Adalbert outside Bohemia, Adalbert being his second name, adopted at his confirmation (reported to be the second) while studying in Magdeburg under the Abbot Adalbert of Magdeburg. It was this Saint Vojtech, who is mentioned as the 'second golden olive after Saint Wenceslas, who will reach seventh heaven by its achievement and will shine in the whole world' in Duchess Libuse's prophecy. He, as a bishop of Prague, asked monk Kristian, who was his nephew, to write in Latin the Legend 'Life and martyrdom of Saint Wenceslas and his grandmother Saint Ludmila' from which I was able to glean some information. The legend is also simply referred to as Kristian's Legend.

Boleslav II and the Premyslids reinforced their control over Bohemia and under their rule the Kingdom of Bohemia prospered. The Premyslids were on the throne for over 300 years and it was not until 1306 that the last Premyslid King, Wenceslas III, was murdered at the age of 17 years in Olomouc, at the beginning of a military expedition to Poland to defend his Polish Crown.

The Czech Crown then shortly passed to the husband of Wenceslas III's oldest sister Ann, Henry of Carinthia and Tyrol. Rudolf Hapsburg, the son of Emperor Albrecht, took the throne by force, but after his death Henry re-established himself on the throne. But he was not very popular with noblemen. A plan was hatched by them and the church dignitaries to arrange a marriage between the youngest sister of Wenceslas III, Eliska (Agnes), then eighteen, and John of Luxembourg, then fourteen, the only son of the Holy Roman Emperor Henry VII. But first young Eliska had to be helped to escape from St George's Convent in Prague Castle to Germany where the wedding took place. Afterwards the couple travelled with a convoy and a huge army to Bohemia and after taking Prague, John of Luxembourg was crowned as the Czech King.

John was a true knight and spent lots of time away from Bohemia in various wars and battles. He found his death on the battlefield of Crecy, supporting the French King,

Philip VI against the English King, Edward III, and his son, the Black Prince. King John was then already blind, but refused to retreat, when it was apparent that the French side was to lose. It was John's wish to die in battle. His son Charles and others tied horses around King John to protect him, before they retreated.

Charles, a Premyslid on his mother's side, although christened as Wenceslas, was actually called Charles in respect for the French King, at whose court he was educated. When Charles returned to Bohemia, he found the Czech royal estates badly neglected and in debt as a result of his father's appetite for war adventures. But he was helped by the Czech nobility and soon the Czech kingdom under his rule enjoyed peace and prosperity. It gained importance as Charles IV was not only the Czech King, but also became the King of Germany and the Holy Roman Emperor. Charles IV established in Prague the first university north of the Alps and started to build St Vitus Cathedral in support of the newly established archbishopric.

After Charles's death, his son Wenceslas IV became the Czech King and after his death, his younger brother Sigismund, who was already the King of Hungary, became the King of Bohemia. Both brothers also held the title of Holy Roman Emperor. Hussite wars brought an end to this dynasty on the Czech throne.

10. WORSHIP AND RESPECT SHOWN FOR SAINT WENCESLAS

The beloved Duke Wenceslas was recognised by his people as a saint for his good deeds, the dedication of his life to Christianity and his martyrdom soon after his death. People talked about many miracles happening in his name and these stories were added to some of the legends.

One such miracle is reported to have happened when the body of St Wenceslas was transferred from its first grave in Boleslav's castle to Prague Castle. According to Kristian's Legend, wagoners got up in the middle of the night and took the body out of the grave and put it on a wagon, as they had been ordered by their Duke Boleslav. On the way to Prague, they came to a swollen stream, with water from melted snow bursting the stream's banks and flowing across the fields and meadows. Spring flooding was, and still is, a very common event in that part of the country. Thus the convoy could not cross the stream and the men went to look for some wood so they could built a bridge. When they returned, they found the wagon with St Wenceslas's body on the other bank of the swollen stream and perfectly dry. The wagoners were amazed by this miracle.

When they reached the Church of St Vitus in Prague Castle, they lit torches and saw that the body of St Wenceslas was untouched by decay and all wounds healed, except the first one which was still open, the one from his brother Boleslav. Singing songs and hymns, they then put the body into a coffin and buried it beside the altar.

Many miracles were reported to have happened near his new grave. In the Kristian's Legend it is said that a woman living in Prague who was blind and disabled came to St Vitus Church and, with her deep belief, prayed by the grave of St Wenceslas. She was miraculously healed. There was also a Frank with both legs paralysed who in a dream saw a man in a white robe telling him to go to Prague to the Church of St Vitus and there, by the grave of blessed Wenceslas the Martyr, he would be healed. The man first ignored this dream but the same man appeared again in his dreams, urging him to go, so he went without further hesitation. He called on merchants who were travelling to Prague and paid them to take him there. When he got to the Church of St Vitus, he threw himself on the floor in front of everybody and prayed for a long time, tears pouring from his eyes. And then as he got up his legs were healed. Many miracles are reported to have happened to prisoners. During his rule, Good King Wenceslas put a considerable effort into improving the justice system, so that it was fair and rid of pagan rough justice, when innocent people were condemned to the gallows from which only death could free them.

One such miracle is reported to have happened during the journey of St Wenceslas's body from Stara Boleslav to Prague. When the convoy reached Prague, the animals stopped by the gallows and would not move. In the prison there were found innocent Christians and once they had been released, the convoy was able to continue to its destination.

Another miracle is reported to have happened to a group of prisoners tied together by iron chains. They were crowded in the local prison, with no hope of ever getting out alive. So they prayed to blessed Wenceslas, for him to take mercy on them and help them in this lamentable situation. The following night the prisoners first heard the sound of a bell and then a peculiar light lit their cell. Suddenly a wooden beam in which their legs were clamped bent like a bow releasing their legs. They saw that God was helping them and having their hope of freedom restored, they cried, "Our God, Father of our Jesus Christ, help us, your servants. We believe in you and the prayers of Saint Wenceslas, who for the love of you was killed." Their iron manacles fell from their necks to the ground, one by one, and there on the floor of the cell, they broke to bits. Released from the prison, the men travelled around the country telling everybody about this miracle.

Several other miracles accredited to St Wenceslas are reported in the Kristian's Legend concerning freed prisoners. However, he also reports that on one occasion people were sceptical about whether it was a miracle or the result of bribing the jailor who took their handcuffs and chains off. People did not want to let the prisoners go free. As people were gathering, it was decided to put the jailkeeper through God's trial. People made a fire and an iron was put in it. The iron was heated until it was white. The jailor was then asked to take the iron from the fire and carry it in his bare hand a considerable distance away to a spot in a field, marked by others. The jailor did not hesitate, took the hot iron and carried it well beyond the marked spot. Thus any doubt was dispelled as the Legend tells us.

The celebration of Saint Wenceslas's feast started sometime after the transfer of his body to Prague Castle and in 985 was already well established. His importance as the first Czech saint and a patron of Bohemia grew. There were churches built and dedicated to him, and his face and name have appeared on coins throughout the centuries in the Kingdom of Bohemia right up to the present day. Indeed the new government of the Czech Republic, which covers the lands of Bohemia, Moravia and part of Selesia, has a 20 crowns coin in circulation with a picture of Saint Wenceslas on his horse.

Fig. 10.1 Two of the first coins with St Wenceslas. (1012-1034), (1108-1125).

1. Sva-tý Vá-cla-ve, vé-vo-do české země,

kně-že náš, pros zá ny Bo-ha, sva-té-ho Ducha!

Ky-ri-e-lei-son. 2. Ne-bes-kéť jest dvorstvo

krás-né, bla-zě to-mu, ktož tam pój-de:

v ži-vot věč-ný, oheň jas-ný sva-té-ho Ducha.

Ky-ri-e-lei-son. 3. Po-mo-ci tvé žá-dá-my,

smi-luj sě nad ná-mi; utěš smut-né, ot-žeň

vše zlé, sva-tý Vá-cla-ve! Ky-ri-e-lei-son.

ENGLISH TRANSLATION

1.
Saint Wenceslas; Duke of Bohemian lands,
Our Prince, Pray to God for us, And to the Holy Spirit.
Kyrie eleison.

2.
Heaven's Court is beautiful, Happy they who enter
Into Life eternal, The shining light of the Holy Spirit.
Kyrie eleison.

3.
We implore thy succour, Have pity upon us,
Console the sad, Drive all ill away, Saint Wenceslas,
Kyrie eleison.

4.
O, Thou Inheritor of Bohemia, Remember thy race, thy people,
Suffer not us, Nor our children to perish, Saint Wenceslas,
Kyrie eleison.

'Kyrie eleison' means 'Lord have mercy' in Latin

Fig. 10.2 The oldest prayer song dedicated to Saint Wenceslas

One of the oldest songs in Bohemia, dating back to the 10th or 11th century, is dedicated to Saint Wenceslas and it is sometimes suggested that it was composed by Bishop Vojtech (known outside Bohemia as St Adalbert). In the days of the Kingdom of Bohemia it was sung not only as a religious song but also as the national anthem. The last verses were added during the Hussite Wars in the early part of the 15th century. Both sides of the conflict, Catholics and Protestants, worshipped St Wenceslas. These words are also on the present coin, freely translated as: "Saint Wenceslas, do not let us or our descendants perish." The tune is very Slavonic.

One of the most important Czech Kings, Charles IV, who was at the same time the German King and Holy Roman Emperor in the 14th century, had a new royal crown made for his coronation as the King of Bohemia, which he dedicated to Saint Wenceslas and which for future generations belonged to the Kingdom of Bohemia and not to the kings. It was only loaned to the individual kings for their coronation by the Archbishop of Bohemia, its guardian. The crown was kept in Saint Vitus Cathedral, and during the time of Charles IV even rested on the skull of Saint Wenceslas. The Saint Wenceslas's crown found its way to Vienna under the rule of Hapsburgs on the Bohemian throne. Its last return to Prague by train was welcomed with rejoicing by the people of Bohemia, who lined the route of the train with bands playing national songs at every station it passed through.

Besides dedicating the Czech Royal Crown to St Wenceslas, Charles IV started to rebuild the basilica of St Vitus into a cathedral with a special chapel dedicated to St Wenceslas, erected over the original Church of St Vitus with the grave of St Wenceslas in it. This chapel is covered with frescoes depicting the life and death of St Wenceslas. Charles IV also gave the impulse for a unique statue of St Wenceslas, still standing in this very important chapel of which more later.

Charles IV also wrote his own legend of the life and death of St Wenceslas. He drew his information from the earlier legends but adds, what might have been a general belief at his time, that Drahomira was also implicated in the murder of her son Wenceslas and that she was then swallowed by the earth as God's punishment. Earlier, it was mentioned that she left the dukedom for ever, never to return, as there are no further reports about her. However, one legend suggests that she went to Croatia, which could have meant the neighbouring dukedom of Croatia in East Bohemia or the area much further south, where today's Croatia is.

Respect for St Wenceslas grew not only in Bohemia but also in Bavaria and Saxony, where he is known as Saint Wenzel. The First Slavonic Legend found its way into Russia and the early Russian liturgy. The name Vyacheslav, Russian for Wenceslas, has been accepted as a Russian first name throughout the centuries. He is also known under same name in Poland. In the not so distant past, Czech settlers built over 40 churches dedicated to Saint Wenceslas in North America. In Italy the name can be found as Vinceslao in early literature and the name was used as a first name in the past in Spain.

The first introduction to St Wenceslas in the Royal Danish family may have been when Dagmar the daughter of the Czech King Otakar I married the Danish King, Valdemar in Lubeck in 1205. But it is in the legend 'Oriente iam sole' from the 13th century, that it is said that the Danish King Erik Plovpenning had a vision of Christ talking to him and asking him to build a church dedicated to St Wenceslas. King Erik did build a monastery and put in it monks of St Benedict's order. According to one report he brought to Denmark relics of St Wenceslas but it was not possible to find where they were put or if a church dedicated to St Wenceslas really existed. After the reformation the abbey King Erik built was demolished and with it were lost any possible answers.

Sadly, King Erik died at the hand of his own brother, like St Wenceslas. There is a Danish legend, in which it is said that King Erik had a vision of St Wenceslas forewarning him of his own death. He was drowned in 1250 and his death is depicted in murals in St Benedict's Church in Ringsted, Denmark, where he was finally buried in 1268, beside Queen Dagmar and other Danish kings and queens buried there.

The first mention of St Wenceslas came to England with the Roman Missal. Some authors suggest that a daughter of Charles IV, Princess Anne of Bohemia, when she married the English King Richard II in January 1382, also brought with her the story of St Wenceslas.

Today, in Britain and the whole English speaking world, St Wenceslas is known as Good King Wenceslas from the Christmas carol written by John Mason Neale in the last century. (See fig. 10.3.)

John Mason Neale was born in London in 1818 to the wife of Reverend Cornelius Neale, a distinguished Cambridge scholar. Both his father and mother were enthusiastic Evangelicals. His father died from consumption while he was still very young. John Mason then went to Sherborne School and in 1836 won an open scholarship to Trinity College, Cambridge.

In Cambridge he took his degree in 1840 and soon shone as a poet winning the Setonian prize for a sacred poem in 1841, and was successful on ten other occasions. He stayed in college as lecturer for some time but wanted to be a priest and to serve in the community. He was ordained in 1842 and soon afterwards he married. Tuberculosis became a major set back for him and he spent three years in Madeira recuperating. When he returned to England he tried to find a place as a priest but nine bishops turned him down, because, while in Cambridge, he had helped to found the Cambridge Camden (later the Ecclesiological) Society for research into new ideas within the Anglican Church, which made him a 'marked' man. In the spring of 1846 he became the warden of Sackville College on annual salary of £27, on which he brought up a family of five. Sackville College in East Grinstead, England was founded by Robert Sackville, Earl of Dorset in 1608 as a home for old people, who were without sufficient means. The post gave Neale plenty of spare time for writing. He remained there till the end of his life. As a priest, he was not allowed to practice for over 16 years until his bishop lifted the prohibition. (See fig. 10.3.)

It was in Sackville College that Neale wrote most of his books, 38 in total. He also wrote many hymns and carols, almost 300. He knew more or less 20 languages and searched on the Continent in libraries and monasteries for old religious hymns, translating some of them from Latin and other languages into English. In the great collection of hymns entitled *Hymns Ancient and Modern* he contributed almost 1/8 of all the songs. As a hymnologist he wanted to revive Christmas as a festival of song and in 1853 published 12 carols. He was responsible for the words, Thomas Helmore for the music. The most famous of these, still sung today are:'Good Christian Men, Rejoice'; 'Christ Was Born on Christmas Day'; 'Wreathe the Holly'; 'Twine the Bay'; and of course 'Good King Wenceslas Looked Out'.

The last carol 'Good King Wenceslas' did not receive many good comments in his lifetime, but it gained popularity due to its delightful tune, taken from an old spring carol which he found in a rare book, a collection of 73 Latin hymns and carols titled: *Piae Cantiones Ecclesiasticae et Scholasti, veterum Episcoporum, in Inclyto Regno Sueciae passim usurpatae.* This book was published in 1582 for the Lutheran Communion in Sweden. Neale commented that similar songs could be found in libraries in Germany, France and England. The words are Neale's original and based on the same legends told in this book.

Neale not only collected and wrote carols but he also organised carol parties in East Grinstead. It is said that on such an occasion, a member of the party who was a teetotaller and vegetarian suggested that in 'Good King Wenceslas' the line:

Bring me flesh and bring me wine

should be altered to:

Bring me milk and bring me bread

John Mason Neale did not comply with this request. The 'Good King Wenceslas' carol is Neale's most popular one. His genius is now recognised and several books have been written about John Mason Neale. In his own time he was awarded D.D. by Harvard and the Metropolitan of the Greek Church publicly praised him. John Mason Neale died of consumption in 1866 at the age of 48.

In 1973 the Royal Mail made the 'Good King Wenceslas' carol the subject of its Christmas stamps. (See fig. 10.5.) I am pleased to show a first day cover for those who may not have seen the stamps before. The Post Office commented in their special issue that John Mason Neale wanted to influence people with means to be more benevolent to those who need help.

The Music to 'Good King Wenceslas'

GOOD KING WENCESLAS

1.   "Good King Wenceslas look'd out
        On the feast of Stephen
        When the snow lay round about
        Deep and Crisp and even."
        "Brightly shone the moon that night
        though the frost was cruel,
        When a poor man came in sight,
        Gath'ring winter fuel."

2.   "Hither, page, and stand by me,
        If thou know'st it, telling
        Yonder peasant, who is he?
        Where, and what his dwelling?"
        "Sire, he lives a good league hence,
        Underneath the mountain;
        Right against the forest fence,
        By St Agnes fountain."

3.   "Bring me flesh and bring me wine,
        Bring me pine logs thither;
        Thou and I will see hime dine,
        When we bear them hither."
        Page and monarch forth they went,
        Onward both together,
        Through the rude winds wild lament,
        And the bitter weather.

4.   "Sire, the night is darker now
        And the wind blows stronger;
        Fails my heart, I know not how,
        I can go no longer."
        "Mark my footsteps, good my page!
        Tread thou in them boldly;
        Thou shall find the winter's rage
        Freeze thy blood less coldly."

5.   "In his master's steps he trod,
        Where the snow lay dinted;
        Heat was in the very sod
        Which the saint had printed.
        Therefore, Christian men, be sure -
        Wealth or rank possessing -
        Ye, who now will bless the poor,
        Shall yourselves find blessing."

Fig. 10.4 The Carol 'Good King Wenceslas'

11. THE LEGEND OF SAINT WENCESLAS AND THE BLANIK'S KNIGHTS

One last legend needs to be told, that of Saint Wenceslas and the Blanik's Knights. It tells us about a prophecy told to King Charles IV.

There is a mountain in Bohemia called Blanik near the river Blanice. Thick forests cover the mountain, where once stood a wooden castle. Among the trees one can see stones where the castle defence walls used to be. But below the walls in the mountain itself, according to this very old legend, sleep armed knights. They are Saint Wenceslas's army, waiting to be called upon in the hour of his people's greatest need.

On the south side and under the rocky top of the mountain Blanik, there is a rock in the shape of an ark and nearby there is reported to be the entrance to the mountain. There is also a stream from which the knights' horses drink, when once in a while they ride out from the mountain at night for exercise, to return to the mountain by daybreak. During such nights, people would hear the mountain forest to be full of the sounds of drums, horns and the thunder of horses' hoofs.

Once upon a time a girl was cutting grass near the mountain Blanik when suddenly a knight stood by her and asked her to go with him to the mountain and sweep the floor there. She was not afraid and went in through the open gate in the mountain. She could see large halls with vaulted ceilings supported on huge pillars and with swords and lances hung on the walls and pillars. There was not a single sound as all the knights sat at stone tables with their heads bent over and sleeping. Their horses with their saddles on stood, also motionless, by mangers along the walls.

Nobody spoke to the girl and so she got on with her job of sweeping the halls. It did not take her long and soon she was finished. Nobody woke up to speak to her, so she went home.

When she got home they asked her where she had been for so long, but the girl could not understand the question. To her it had all happened in just one day, but she was really surprised when they told her that she had been away for exactly one year. So she told them what had happened and they understood. However, the girl unfortunately died three days later, never to tell her tale again.

On another occasion, a smith from the nearby village of Lounovice was asked by an unknown knight to go into the mountain of Blanik and shoe the horses. When he finished, they gave him a sack full of dust on the way out. He was insulted by this and emptied the sack outside the gate. When he got home, he was told that his family had already shed tears for him, as he had disappeared without a trace exactly a year ago. He told them what had happened and then shook the sack and three golden coins fell out. He realised what a mistake he had made and ran to the gate in the rock, but there was no sign of golden coins or even the dust he shook out of his sack.

There is also talk of a shepherd who was looking for his sheep and found himself in the mountain Blanik for one year without realising it. Even today, the mountain Blanik, some 50km from Prague is still swathed in mystery.

What about the prophecy? The prophecy was that when the most difficult time comes for Saint Wenceslas's people, when their country is torn by fighting, the mountain will open and Saint Wenceslas on his white horse will ride out from the mountain leading the Blanik's Knights into battle to bring them everlasting peace.

I always believed that the amazing story of Good King Wenceslas, how he lived and ruled in his very difficult and changing times, would move people's hearts and bring respect for him and his ideals.

The last upheaval in Bohemia, that of splitting Czechoslovakia into independent Czech and Slovak Republics went through peacefully and thus the story of Good King Wenceslas and his Blanik's Knights have a new mission, to move people's hearts in the trouble spots of the world, where brother stands against brother, neighbour against neighbour, nation against nation and to bring them hope of everlasting peace with dignity. (See fig. 11.1, 11.2, 11.3.)

PART II - PLACES OF INTEREST

12. PRAGUE AND PRAGUE CASTLE

Early History

Archaeological finds indicate that the hilly left-hand bank of the river Vltava was inhabited from the very early days of mankind, while the right bank was not inhabited until much later, because it was prone to flooding. On the left bank there have been finds from the Old Stone Age through the New Stone Age, Bronze Age, Iron Age and the Celtic culture of the 4th century BC. At one time Germanic tribes inhabited the area and there have been archaeological finds of their iron furnaces, just below the castle in the Little Quarter Square, which fall into the 4th century AD. At the end of the 5th century, Slavonic tribes started to move in from the east and north.

The castle was founded in the late 9th century on a headland above the valley of the river Vltava by Duke Borivoj, the grandfather of Good King Wenceslas. It became his seat and that of the other Czech dukes and kings who followed him, replacing Levy Hradec, the place from which Borivoj and his predecessors had previously ruled Central Bohemia.

In those days it was customary to fortify castles by earthen ramparts. Prague Castle had natural defences with steep hills on two sides and artificially dug moats on the other two. It was not until Duke Bretislav I (ruled 1000-1055) that they were replaced by stone fortifications.

From archaeological excavations it is obvious that at the time of Good King Wenceslas most of the buildings, including the duke's residence, were still made of wood, while stone was used for the churches, built in the Roman style. There is very little left of these buildings except foundations underneath the existing courtyards and buildings. Also the boundaries have changed slightly, as you can see by comparing the drawing of the original layout with the later phases of the castle up to the present day. (See fig. 12.1.)

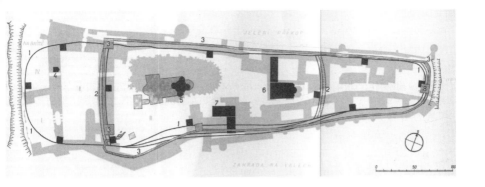

1. Fortifications from 9th & 10th century 2. Moat and rampart
3. Stone wall from the year 1042 4. Church of St Mary
5. St Vitus Rotunda 6. Church of St George
7. Ducal palace 8. Black tower

Fig. 12.1 Layout of Prague Castle through the ages by Ivan Borkovsky

The first Religious Buildings in Prague Castle

It was in Levy Hradec that the first church in Bohemia, dedicated to St Clement, was built by Borivoj and Ludmila. The second church in Bohemia, dedicated to St Mary, was built on the site of a pagan altar, before the hill was fortified to form the new Prague Castle. (See fig. 12.4.) Both churches were built in the Roman style and were very small, able to take only a limited number of worshippers. We must assume that most worshippers would have stood outside the church during services. Most castles of that period acquired two or three small churches. Only the foundations remain of St Mary's Church today.

As building techniques developed, larger churches were being built. The second church built within the boundaries of Prague Castle was dedicated to St George. It was founded in 920 by Duke Vratislav I, the father of Good King Wenceslas. It was outside this church that the young Wenceslas was installed on his dukal seat. It was to this church that Wenceslas had the remains of his beloved grandmother Ludmila transferred from Tetin Castle.

In 973, the first convent in Bohemia was established by Duke Boleslav II and his sister Princess Mlada, beside the Church of St George. The church was converted and enlarged into a Romanesque basilica, which remains there today and forms one of the best preserved relics of Romanesque architecture in Bohemia. Princess Mlada became the first abbess of the convent. In the reconstruction of the basilica in 1142, two towers were added. Late in the 17th century, an Early Baroque front was built, fronting the Romanesque basilica.

During an archaeological dig carried out in 1958-62, the oldest masonry of Vratislav's St George's Church was unearthed below the floor-level of the present Basilica of

33

St George. Graves of the first Czech dukes from the Premyslid dynasty were also excavated. It was found that both the first church and the basilica stood on shallow foundations carved in slate.

St George's Convent kept an important criptorium throughout the middle ages. Numerous outstanding illuminated manuscripts, musical manuscripts and works of art originated from there. In 1782 the convent was abolished and converted into barracks. In 1962-72 it became an art gallery.

St Vitus Cathedral
The St Vitus Rotunda, built by Good King Wenceslas some time between the years 925 and 935, stood for over a hundred years (fig.4.1). It was later demolished and replaced by a triple-naved Romanesque basilica dedicated to St Vitus, St Wenceslas and St Adalbert and built by Duke Spytihnev in 1060-96. Today, the foundations and masonry of the rotunda and the basilica have been made accessible in the area beneath the present cathedral.

When the Prague bishopric was raised to an archbishopric, the Czech King Charles IV laid the foundations of a new Gothic cathedral in 1344 in the place of the basilica. The cathedral was dedicated to St Vitus, with separate chapels dedicated to St Adalbert and St Wenceslas.

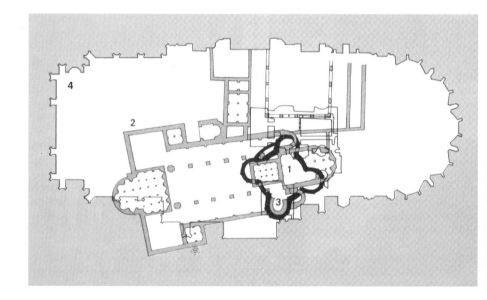

Fig. 12.6 Projected plans of the three buildings (by Petr Chotebor):
1. The foundations of the St Vitus Rotunda
2. The foundations of the St Vitus, St Wenceslas and St Adalbert Basilica
3. The grave of St Wenceslas
4. The present Cathedral of St Vitus

The cathedral was originally designed by a French architect, Matthias of Arras, who supervised the construction for eight years until 1352. Peter Parler of Gmund in Swabia (today's Germany) continued the construction and he also changed the original design. Peter Parler died in 1399 and his work was continued by his sons, John and Wenceslas until the Hussite Wars. The work on the cathedral was halted by the Hussite Wars after the death of King Wenceslas IV, the son of Emperor Charles IV. Later, when the castle was occupied by Hussites, the cathedral was damaged.

New work started during the reign of King Vladislav Jagiellon in 1509, when the foundations were laid for the north tower and the pillars of the main nave. Bonifac Wohlmunt completed the spire of the main tower in a Renaissance style in 1562.

During the Rebellion of the Estates in 1619, the Calvinists plundered the cathedral and changed it into a prayer house. In 1673 new steps were taken to complete the cathedral. In 1861 the 'Union for the Completion of the Cathedral' was formed and over three generations, when it was led by Josef Kranner, Josef Mocker and Kamil Hilbert, the cathedral was first repaired and then finally completed by 1929, some 585 years after Charles IV laid its foundation stone and over 1000 years after Good King Wenceslas laid the foundation stone for his rotunda in that very place.

The year 1929 was a very special year. It was decided to celebrate the millennium of St Wenceslas's martyrdom and major religious as well as national celebrations took place, in which the St Vitus Cathedral with its St Wenceslas Chapel played a major role.

The cathedral is 60 metres (197 feet) wide, 124 metres (407 feet) long and 33 metres (108 feet) high. The main tower is only a few centimetres short of 100 metres (328 feet). There are portraits and statues of saints, members of the royal family and the architects and contributors to the cathedral from the Masters of Parler's workshops to the artists of the 20th century.

The Royal Crypt, in which can be seen the sarcophagi of Charles IV and other Czech kings, is accessible to visitors.

St Wenceslas Chapel

The new cathedral had a chapel dedicated to St Wenceslas and built above the former Wenceslas's St Vitus Rotunda, where his second grave had been since AD 938. St Wenceslas Chapel is unique in that it has two heavy doors at its two entrances. These doors symbolise the wooden doors outside which Wenceslas was killed in Stara Boleslav. The doors are closed every evening and remain closed until the next morning to symbolise the closed doors which denied him the sanctuary of a holy church.

The St Wenceslas Chapel was founded in 1362-7 and is the work of Peter Parler. The lower part of the walls are clad with over 1300 precious stones: red jasper, purple amethyst and green chrysoprase laid out in the constantly repeated motif of a cross. The upper walls of this Gothic chapel are covered by paintings depicting the legends of St Wenceslas, in which he delivers wood to widows, visits prisoners, feeds hungry travellers, buries the dead, officiates during the mass, advises Podiven to follow in his footsteps in the snow, ploughs a field, sows corn, harvests and threshes corn, makes wine and bakes bread for religious purposes, meets King Henry the Fowler of Saxony and receives from him relics of St Vitus and then places them in the altar of his rotunda, arranges a duel with Duke Radslav of Kourim and receives his subordination, goes to Boleslav's castle in Stara Boleslav and is finally killed there. There is also a painting of how Podiven avenges his master's death and is hung for it. One painting shows the Danish King Erik Plovpenning being commanded by Christ to build a church dedicated to St Wenceslas. Another shows him inspecting the completed church. Some paintings are from 1372-3 while others are from the early part of the 16th century.

A unique position in the chapel is taken by the polychrome Gothic statue of St Wenceslas. It is believed to have been made by Peter Parler's nephew Henry Parler in 1373.

When it was carefully examined in the recent past and the head was compared with the actual skull of St Wenceslas, it was concluded that the artist must have used the skull to recreate St Wenceslas's head with its facial features, making this statue unique. It must be one of the earliest of such restorations surviving today. Such methods are more commonly associated with present-day scientists than with mediaeval artists. If we ask ourselves what Good King Wenceslas really looked like then this statue is the closest answer we have today.

It is known that the grave was opened during the reign of Charles IV and at the time of construction of the chapel and so it can be concluded that the artist had St Wenceslas's skull and other bones to help him with his statue. The statue is 2 metres (6ft 6 in) tall.

Scientists examining the few bones left today, have concluded that St Wenceslas was strongly built and must have been trained in arms from an early age.

During a close examination of his skull, a small fraction of blonde or light brown hair was found attached to it. This, if it can be relied on, contradicts a past general assumption that he had dark hair, as on most paintings he is painted with dark hair. This was based on legends about the original Czech people as confirmed by Ibrahim ibn Jacob, who visited Bohemia during the rule of Boleslav I in 965-6. His report is included in the 'Books of Journeys and Countries' by Spanish-Arabic geographer Abu Obaid al-Bakri, who died in Cordoba in 1094. Ibrahim ibn Jacob says: 'People in Boleslav's country had dark hair and tanned complexions while people with blond hair and light complexions were not frequent.' Although this confirms that the majority of people had dark hair it however does not exclude the possibility that Saint Wenceslas had blond or light brown hair and only future scientific analysis will be able to tell us for sure. (See fig. 12.7.)

The age of Saint Wenceslas was also scientifically estimated from his bones and teeth in 1977 and concluded to be about 40 plus/minus several years. If we assume the year 907 as correct for his birth and the year 935 as correct for his death then his age could have been 28, which is at the lower end of the anthropological estimate.

Development of Prague Castle Today

We can only reconstruct the layout from archaeological excavations in Prague and elsewhere. The typical fortification wall was made of stone laid on the outside, with anchoring wooden posts behind it forming a mesh. This was filled with soil. (See fig. 12.8.)

The typical buildings of that time were of wooden log construction.

The fortified hill top was divided by Borivoj into three parts (fig. 12.1.) to provide more protection for the central part, where the duke's palace was. There was also a mint during Boleslav's rule and the churches of St Vitus and St George. Accommodation for servants, soldiers, priests and noblemen was across all three parts of the castle. Stables for horses and other domestic animals were also present.

The duke's palace was based on foundations formed by stones laid without mortar. The ground floor would have been covered by tiles. The walls were made of logs. The palace had one floor above the ground with windows and possibly a balcony.

A mention of the palace is found in Cosmas's description of the enthronement ceremony of Duke Bretislav I. There it is said that coins were thrown though the grilles of the upper windows of the palace to people waiting below.

In 1003 the castle was occupied by the Polish ruler Boleslav Chrabry, a Premyslid by his mother. In 1004 it was retaken by the Czech Premyslid Jaromir with the help of Emperor Henry II.

In the reign of Duke Bretislav I, in 1041, Emperor Henry III besieged Prague Castle with his troops and burnt it down. After the defeat, Bretislav completely rebuilt the fortifications from the original stone and earthen ramparts into walls and towers laid in stone and mortar in the Roman style.

The next major Romanesque reconstruction of Prague Castle is connected with Duke Sobeslav, who after 1135 had built new stone walls, which were up to 14 metres high in places, strengthened by four square towers: the White Tower by the western gate, the Black Tower by the eastern gate, the southern tower and the tower of Burgrave's Residence.

The reconstruction was completed by Duke, later King Vladislav II. During his rule the castle was besieged, but successfully defended. The struggle for the throne and the castle left the castle in constant need of repair.

During the rule of the Czech Kings Premysl Otakar I and Wenceslas I, the Kingdom of Bohemia flourished and with it Prague Castle.

After the death of the last Premyslid king, Wenceslas III, in 1306, the castle fell into disrepair, due to the struggle for the throne and later to its neglect by King John of Luxembourg.

It was the son of John of Luxembourg, Charles IV, who, as the Margrave of Moravia, had already started to rebuild Prague Castle. The work continued when he became the King of Bohemia and later Emperor. Prague Castle became his imperial residence. The newly built St Vitus Cathedral contained the St Wenceslas Chapel, in which St Wenceslas's tomb was heavily plated with gold.

His son, King Wenceslas IV continued to make improvements to the castle. But after his death, at the time of the Hussite Wars, the castle was looted by the people of Prague. In 1420, the younger son of Charles IV, Sigismund, was crowned there as the Czech King. In the afternoon after the coronation, Sigismund's men removed all the gold and silver from St Vitus Cathedral, including the St Wenceslas Chapel and St Wenceslas's tomb. The precious metals were then used to make coins to pay Sigismund's soldiers. Sigismund promised to make better decorations and ornaments once times were more settled in Bohemia, but this never happened.

After the Hussite Wars, Prague Castle was not used by the kings as a residence, instead they used the Royal Court in the town.

It was the popular uprising of 1483 which forced the Czech King Vladislav Jagiello of Poland to start to repair Prague Castle and the rebuilding continued during the rule of King Louis Jagiello. The death of Louis, King of Bohemia and Hungary, in the Battle of Mohacs in 1526 ended the reign of the Jagiello dynasty. The new King of Bohemia was Ferdinand Hapsburg, the husband of Ludvik's sister Anna. He at first resided in Prague Castle, but later it was Queen Anna and the governor - Archduke Ferdinand Tyrol - who represented him there.

Reconstruction of the castle began in the Renaissance style. A new Royal Garden and Summer Palace were built on the northern side of the castle. A wooden bridge on huge stone pillars was built across the gorge between the castle and the new Royal Gardens.

A major fire in 1541, which destroyed Prague's Little Quarter below the castle, as well as the castle itself and the adjacent town of Hradcany, accelerated the reconstruction of the castle in the Renaissance style. (See fig. 12.9.)

Emperor Rudolf II was a keen builder and a collector of the arts. He built a new northern wing with two big halls over the stables of his Spanish horses. These are still called the Spanish Hall and the Rudolph Gallery.

When in 1612 Matthias succeeded Rudolph as the Czech King and as Emperor, he made his imperial residence in Vienna. Despite that, more work was done in the Early Baroque style in the Garden of Paradise and the Garden on the Rampants. The present western gate to the castle falls into this period and is now called Matthias Gate.

During the Thirty Years' War, which started with the defenestration of the Catholic governors from Prague Castle in 1618, the castle was occupied in 1631 by Saxon troops and later in 1648 by Swedish troops.

Destruction and looting occurred in both instances. After the war, the castle was again repaired and Emperor Leopold I restarted the work on St Vitus Cathedral and a riding-school was founded outside the castle.

In 1723, when Emperor Charles VI was crowned as the Czech King, some interiors of the royal palace were restyled. More stables were added to those already present.

A major reconstruction took place during the rule of Empress Maria Theresa. During her rule, Prague was occupied by French and Saxon allied troops in 1741, and in 1744 and 1757 by the Prussian army and as a result of this, the castle was damaged by gunfire.

Afterwards, during the reconstruction, the outside of this mediaeval-looking castle was transformed into its present appearance.

During the rule of Joseph II, the castle suffered many setbacks. Joseph II had no understanding of art or history, and virtually all the art treasures and precious items of the national heritage were lost for ever at a series of auctions. The ruler also gave the army several important buildings within the castle, namely St George's Convent, the Royal Summer Palace, a big games hall and the riding-school. These were damaged by unsuitable usage.

In 1848, the resigning Emperor Ferdinand V made Prague Castle his retirement residence. During the preparation for the coronation of the Emperor Franz Joseph I as the Czech King, the Spanish Hall and Rudolf Gallery were redecorated. However, neither this nor any other coronation of the Hapsburg rulers ever took place, to the disappointment of the Czech people.

The St Wenceslas's Crown of the Kingdom of Bohemia, used for coronations since Charles IV's coronation, was never used for its purpose again. Prague and Prague Castle lost in importance to Vienna.

The sun set on the Austro-Hungarian empire with the end of the First World War. Republics rose along the lines of the kingdoms: Austria, Hungary and Czechoslovakia. Slovakia left Hungary to join the Czechs and Moravians in Czechoslovakia.

With the birth of Czechoslovakia in 1918, the castle became the seat of the presidents and the centre of the republic. Restoration over several decades made the castle a jewel of the nation. From 1 January 1993, when Czechoslovakia split peacefully into Slovakia and the Czech Republic of Bohemia and Moravia, Prague Castle has been the seat of the president of the Czech Republic: Vaclav Havel, who led the Velvet Revolution in 1989 which brought back democracy.

Wenceslas Square in the City of Prague

When talking about Prague Castle it is not possible to ignore the City of Prague below the castle itself and, particularly Wenceslas Square. Wenceslas Square was known before 1848 as the Horse Market and the purpose of the lower part from its foundation was for trading horses and other commodities. With its many stalls and open shops it formed a commercial centre of the town. The upper part of the square was on the outskirts of the New Town and in its part had the gallows and local inns for coachmen and travellers. The New Town, with its spacious layout was boldly founded in 1348 by the Czech King Charles IV.

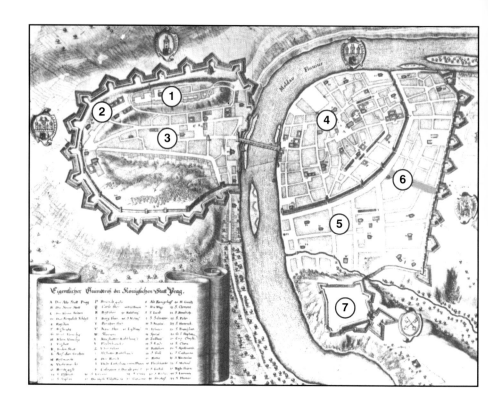

Fig 12.10 Map of Prague in 1652. 1. Prague Castle 2. Hradcany 3. Lesser Town 4. Old Town 5. New Town 6. Horse Market - today's Wenceslas Square 7. Vysehrad

A fountain with the statue of St Wenceslas on his horse was positioned in the middle part of what was the Horse Market in 1680 during the reign of King Leopold I. As a plague in 1713 prevented meetings in Prague churches, open air mass services were held by the statue. A legend, originating from the Middle Ages, tells us about a mysterious knight (Good King Wenceslas) riding on a white horse and commanding the gate keeper at the top of the square to open the gates before disappearing into the night. The next day he would assist Bohemian soldiers in battle wherever they needed help.

In 1827 the statue was transferred to the upper part of the square and in 1848 the square itself was renamed Wenceslas Square according to the Czech patriotic writer Karel Havlicek Borovsky (see fig. 12.11 first statue of St Wenceslas on his horse). In 1848 an open air mass took place in front of the statue and the Czech national requirements were read aloud, before Prague erupted in an armed uprising which was only to be suppressed after five days of fighting by Austrian soldiers stationed in Prague Castle, led by General Windischgraet.

In 1879 the original statue of St Wenceslas, created by Jan Jiri Bendl, was moved to Vysehrad. The present statue of St Wenceslas on his horse and surrounded by the statues of four Czech Saints (Ludmila, Agnes, Adalbert and Procopius) was erected in its place in 1912. The memorial was the work of sculptor Josef Vaclav Myslebeck, who won a national competition for the monument held in 1894.

The statue witnessed the birth of Czechoslovakia on 28 October 1918, when people assembled around it and listened to the Czech speakers celebrating the proclamation of the new state.

Wenceslas Square, being the main square in Prague, also bore witness to sad times, during the Second World War and again in 1968 when Soviet tanks rolled over Wenceslas Square and destroyed the Prague Spring. In November 1989, Wenceslas Square and the statue again became a centre for protest and assemblies rallying for the re-establishment of democracy.

Today, the statue of St Wenceslas looks down on Wenceslas Square, witnessing happier times. The statue itself is often the place for the laying of flowers and wreaths by visiting statesmen from abroad. (See fig. 12.12.)

13. STARA BOLESLAV

Boleslav's castle

Boleslav's castle was situated along a well known trading route leading from Prague to the Baltic Sea. It guarded a ford across the river Elbe (Labe in Czech). It is documented by archaeological finds that settlements were frequently found along this route. On the other side of the river, where today's town of Brandys Nad Labem (Brandys on Elbe) is situated, archaeological finds indicate settlements well into the 4th and 3rd Century BC. The establishment of what became known as Boleslav's castle along the trading route on the banks of the rivers Elbe and Jizera is attributed to Duke Spytihnev, the uncle of princes Wenceslas and Boleslav. There are no written records to support this but the age of the castle can be judged from archaeological finds.

The castle was naturally protected on three sides by the two rivers and marshland created by them and on the fourth side by deep forests. The castle was situated on an important trading route, then on the border of the Czech Dukedom. When it was no longer a border castle it became a hunting lodge. The tradition of royal hunting in these forests persisted well into the 18th century, when the Hapsburgs made use of their castle on the other side of the river Elbe in Brandys.

After the death of Duke Vratislav I in 921, when Wenceslas took power, his younger brother Boleslav was given this castle to live in so that he could administer the adjoining land under the rule of Wenceslas. The castle, with time, took on Boleslav's name and that part of the country was referred to in some old documents as Boleslavia.

According to Cosmas, Prince Boleslav was defiant towards Wenceslas and for this reason he decided to fortify his castle well. Cosmas tells how Boleslav assembled the elders of this land and asked them to build the castle walls in the Roman style.

When their spokesman replied to Boleslav that they did not know how to do it and anyway they did not want to do it, Boleslav, without hesitation cut this man's head off and thus broke their resistance at once. Boleslav then had the walls of his castle built in stone in the Roman style. It was thought that this story was invented by Cosmas to spice up his writings, which are known as the 'Cosmas Chronicle'.

However, in 1993, local archaeologists, led by Jaroslav Spacek, dug along the wall of the formal castle and found several walls. The first was of stone laid without mortar, while the second one was built with mortar in the Roman style, thus confirming at least part of the story. (See fig. 13.6.) This story and that of the killing of his brother Wenceslas made historians and writers refer to Boleslav until very recently as Boleslav the Cruel. In current publications he is being referred to as Boleslav I, and his son and grandson, who ruled the country after him, are known as Boleslav II and Boleslav III.

There is another castle further east on the river Jizera, now called Mlada (Young) Boleslav. It is not certain whether this second castle was established by Boleslav I himself before 950 or by his son Boleslav II after the year 995.

Thus some time after the second castle was built, Boleslav's castle with the adjoining settlements on the river Elbe became known as Stara (Old) Boleslav and the other castle and settlements further east on the river Jizera were first referred to as Novy (New) Boleslav, and from the 14th century on as Mlada (Young) Boleslav.

A brief history of this castle in Mlada Boleslav tells us that according to Widukind, a peace agreement between Boleslav I and the Emperor Otto I, after fourteen years of war, was agreed below an encircled settlement, known as 'urbs Nova', New Town. Also another paper from that time, when a number of Royal Courts were given to a convent in Regensburg, was signed by Otto I on 16 July 950 in 'beheim suburbio Niwnburg', translated as in 'Bohemia outside New Castle'. This would confirm that a castle in Mlada Boleslav was indeed established during the rule of Boleslav I. But there are historians who argue that Boleslav I and the Premyslids could not have built such a castle on the border with the powerful Slavniks before 995.

Beside the perimeter wall of the St Wenceslas Basilica in Stara Boleslav is a statue of a lion (see fig. 13.5) which one historian suggests was put in the position where a throne for Otto I was built, when Boleslav I agreed peace with him. This story was supported by Palacky, an important Czech historian.

Boleslav's castle on the river Elbe had its walls built in the Roman style, a style new to Bohemia, while Prague and other castles were built in the old Slavonic style. It may have been because of these new walls and no doubt other new buildings within Boleslav's castle also in the Roman style, that Boleslav's castle in Stara Boleslav may have been referred to as 'urbs Nova' if the second castle in Mlada (Young) Boleslav did not yet exist. But even that cannot be conclusive because other suggestions are offered about the story that an emperor's throne once stood in Stara Boleslav.

In another historical suggestion, it was the Holy Roman Emperor Konrad II, who fought a war against the Czech duke, Oldrich, whose son Bretislav carried away a nun from a convent and married her. Her name was Judith and she was a sister of Frankish Margrave Otto. Judith, with her eloquent tongue, arranged a peace between Konrad II, her brother Otto and her husband, the Czech Prince Bretislav. Emperor Konrad II then ordered that a throne should be built for him in the centre of Bohemia, in Boleslav's castle of Stara Boleslav, to seal the peace.

Another story suggests that it was a successor of Konrad, the Emperor Henry III, who went to Bohemia with a great army and vowed to have a throne built in the centre of Bohemia in the same castle in Stara Boleslav, after Duchess Judith had negotiated peace between him and her husband Duke Bretislav. Yet another possible suggestion is that Duke Bretislav brought home from a military expedition to Poland a golden throne of Charles the Great, given by the Emperor Otto III to the Polish ruler as thanks for sending him relics of Saint Adalbert. Bretislav then gave the throne, among other foundation gifts, to the new Basilica of St Wenceslas in Stara Boleslav.

That a throne was still in Stara Boleslav at the end of the 13th century and the beginning of the 14th century is supported by Dalimil in his Chronicle. The actual statue of a lion was put there some time between 1682 and 1695 by Provost Jan A. Capek, in the place where a white stone marked the position of the throne. A lion was a symbol of the Kingdom of Bohemia and placing it there must have been a national encouragement for the Czech pilgrims visiting Stara Boleslav. The Battle on White Mountain in 1620 started the Thirty Years' War when many lives were lost. Many Protestants - noblemen, town citizens and peasants from villages alike - left the country and Bohemia was governed from Vienna.

Some excavations in Stara Boleslav, early in the present century, indicate that there were two or three great fires during the history of the castle which destroyed some, if not all, of the buildings. Some of the buildings were built of wood and some of stone. Further archaeological excavations would be needed to shed more light on the history of this castle. This has not been easy as Old Boleslav Castle has always been inhabited, once it had stopped being a castle. The church and civilians built on the grounds of the former castle. Thus archaeologists today can only excavate alongside public works like the laying down of new gas or water pipes.

There are historical reports that Czech dukes and kings stayed in the Old Boleslav Castle. The castle was strengthened in 1350 by the Emperor and Czech King Charles IV with new walls and castle gates, one of which still remains today.

During the Hussite Wars the castle at first remained loyal to the king and thus we learn that King Sigismund stayed there in May 1420 with his wife, Queen Barbora and Zofia, the widow of his brother Wenceslas IV. They moved out on 27 May and went to Melnik. Prague citizens, who were on the side of the Protestants, had taken Old Boleslav Castle in December 1420. The Lord of Michalovic retook it and the castle was in alliance with King Sigismund from April to October 1421. The Hussite army from Prague took it again after a tough battle and by 4 October they returned singing victoriously to Prague.

Although there are no specific records to document it, it is assumed that the castle, with its King's Palace, was destroyed by a fire and never rebuilt. The west gate, similar to the present east gate, was lost. I remember people saying that the remains of the west gate were visible in the water of the moat. I tried to look for them on sunny days without success.

The new bigger walls built by Charles IV remained in places. There are reports that in 1433 the castle was still in the hands of Prague Hussites.

As the castle was not rebuilt after the Hussite Wars, it lost its importance as a place for royalty but gradually gained religious status, and pilgrims travelled to Stara Boleslav from all over the country. The grounds were used by the church for their accommodation and by civilians for their businesses. In reading historical books I found that my great grandfather, Augustine Rejzl, was in the last century a master shoemaker just inside the castle boundaries by the eastern gate in what later became a pub called 'U Modre Hvezdy', 'By a Blue Star'.

Churches in the grounds of Boleslav's castle
The Church of St Clement was built in the Roman style in the grounds of the castle and can be dated to the days of Wenceslas's father Vratislav. It is assumed to be one of the oldest buildings in Bohemia and remains there still today.

It is sometimes suggested that it was built in place of a wooden church established there by the Moravian missionaries or their pupils. It was a custom of the Moravian missionaries to establish churches dedicated to St Clement in important places along the route of their missions and travel. The first church built in Bohemia, in Levy Hradec by Borivoj was dedicated to St Clement. Churches were also established by the missionaries Cyril and Methodius and their pupils and dedicated to St Clement throughout Moravia and Pannonia (a western part of Hungary). But it has not been archaeologically proved that the St Clement Church in Stara Boleslav belongs to this group. Another suggestion exists that the church may actually be much younger and from the 11th century.

During an excavation in 1993 in the grounds of the castle, foundations were found of another church built in stone, dating from the 11th century. It must have been built on shallow foundations, because it is apparent from the excavation that the walls collapsed during flooding by the rivers. The church was never rebuilt. There is no known name for this church and no mention of its existence. All the church records were taken abroad during the Hussite Wars, as the priest left for Zittau in Germany and the records were never returned.

The church at the door of which Good King Wenceslas was killed by his assassins, was dedicated to the Saints Cosmas and Damian, as legends tell us. It is not certain if this was of wooden structure at first and later replaced by a church built of stone. This may possibly have been the present Vrabska Chapel, later added to a new design of a basilica dedicated to St Wenceslas and a crypt, to which the dedication to Saints Cosmas and Damian was transferred.

Some earlier suggestions are that the first part of the crypt is the remainder of the Church of Saints Cosmas and Damian, while the front part of the crypt was called the Bretislav's Crypt, because it is assumed that it was added by him, while the Vrabska Chapel was built over the place of martyrdom of St Wenceslas.

The crypt and basilica may have been built with the place of St Wenceslas's first grave as their central axis or the official grave may have been placed at their centre later. The original complex was built by Duke Bretislav I as a penance ordered by Pope Benedict IX after Bretislav's military expedition to Poland in 1039.

The story behind Bretislav's basilica of St Wenceslas

It had long been a wish of the Czech dukes to establish an archbishopric in Prague. The Polish King Boleslav Chrabry had achieved this aim in the year 1000 at the site of the grave of St Adalbert in Gneizdno, Poland. Bretislav believed that bringing home to Prague the relics of St Adalbert, an internationally respected Czech saint who had found his martyrdom in a foreign land, would make his application to Rome for an archbishopric in Prague successful. Bretislav therefore took advantage of confusion in Poland and marched his army deep into the country to occupy Gneizdno, the capital, in 1039.

Bishop Sebir of Prague, who had travelled with Bretislav's army, served a special mass over the open grave of St Adalbert as Duke Bretislav laid down the first written laws. Bretislav's Dekrets (decrees) were based on the principles which St Adalbert had preached so energetically, including the permanence of monogamous marriage, the celebration of Sunday as a holy day with no work taking place and the burying of people in Christian cemeteries. Bretislav set stiff penalties for disobeying his Dekrets, for example, for having more than one wife, burying people according to pagan practices in fields and forests, murder, alcoholism and for selling alcohol without a licence.

Bretislav not only brought back with him relics of St Adalbert, relics of his brother Radim and those of the five Polish Holy Bretheren, but also the looted gold, silver and precious ornaments and relics normally associated with such military expeditions in those days. It was reported that the loot was carried back in one hundred heavy wagons. Cattle and prisoners - slaves were also taken back to Prague. Cosmas, the first Czech chronicler, claims that his forefather was among them.

Bretislav sent a delegation to the Pope to explain that he had taken the relics of St Adalbert under his protection and that he wanted to establish an archbishopric in Prague. But a Polish messenger got to Rome before Bretislav's delegation from Bohemia and told Pope Benedict IX what had happened. Thus when the Czech delegation arrived, it was put on the defensive and had to accept a penance order for Bretislav to establish a new monastery. What is more, Prague was not raised to an archbishopric for another 305 years.

Thus Bretislav, instead of a monastery, chose to build a basilica dedicated to St Wenceslas on the site of his death and his first grave in Stara Boleslav. We do not know what the original basilica looked like or how it was laid out. It was built in the Roman style and was consecrated on 18 May 1046 by the Bishop of Prague, Sebir.

In 1052, a deanery was established beside the basilica of Saint Wenceslas and the duke gave the whole of the north and north-east side of the castle for its use. In Latin writings of the time this Boleslav's castle was already called Old Boleslav, i.e. Boleslavia Antigua or Boleslavia Vetus.

The present basilica is exceptionally large and its plan view falls into the rebuilding period in the 12th century. It enclosed the crypt dedicated to the Saints Cosmas and Damian and what was called 'Vrabska' Chapel (named after the noble family of Vrabi; Vrabi is now part of Brandys). There are Roman windows hidden underneath the roof of the Vrabska Chapel, suggesting its origins in the early times of Roman style and possibly its being the much taller structure of an independent church. This is why some experts suggest that it may have been the original Church of the Saints Cosmas and Damian. This suggestion cannot be ruled out until thorough archaeological and historical analysis is done.

During the Hussite Wars the priests left for Zittau and the St Wenceslas Basilica was burnt down. It was later rebuilt in the Gothic style, but did not reach its full glory until 1593. It is still visible in places that the round Roman arches between the main pillars were filled in to form Gothic arches. The present ceilings of the side naves and the outside supporting pillars date from this restoration.

But it was not long before the basilica suffered again. During the Thirty Years' War, which started in 1618, it was used as stables by the Swedish army. The north tower was demolished by them for military purposes. As the army retreated, the basilica and the Church of St Clement were accidentally set alight.

After this war, the basilica was again repaired and the main nave was given its present ceiling. The remaining tower was finished by roofing in the Baroque style.

Stara Boleslav flourished as a main pilgrimage site in the Kingdom of Bohemia. All those visiting Prague also visited Stara Boleslav. Small chapels were built all the way along the route from the St Wenceslas Chapel in Prague Castle to St Wenceslas Basilica in Stara Boleslav. The chapels were put up between 1680 and 1690 to mark the holy journey St Wenceslas undertook before his death. They were 400 metres (1312 ft.) apart, which is the length of the Charles Bridge in Prague. Individual noble families financed them and their coats of arms and names were on their sides. The chapels were decorated with paintings depicting scenes from St Wenceslas's life and death. Some chapels can still be seen along the route, at times in the middle of fields, as the route of the road has changed through the centuries. (See fig. 13.7.)

There are not many of these chapels left and even less have the original paintings in them. For those interested, the paintings were as follows, starting with the first chapel on the way from Prague Castle: 1. St Mary being worshipped by St Ludmila and St Wenceslas 2. The making of the picture of St Mary (later referred to as Palladium) from smelted statues of pagan gods given by St Ludmila 3. St Wenceslas as a baby being passed to St Ludmila 4. Priest Paul teaching St Wenceslas 5. St Wenceslas assisting during a holy mass 6. Drahomira expelling priests 7. St Wenceslas being enthroned 8. St Wenceslas forbidding the worship of pagan gods 9. The death of St Ludmila 10. St Wenceslas buying young children out of slavery 11.

St Wenceslas cutting corn, harvesting wheat and preparing bread 12. St Wenceslas pressing grapes to make wine 13. St Wenceslas attending the funeral of poor people 14. St Wenceslas predicting his martyrdom 15. St Wenceslas delivering wood to the poor 16. St Wenceslas having the relics of St Ludmila transferred to Prague 17. St Wenceslas winning over Radslav of Kourim 18. St Wenceslas founding a hospice for poor people beside the gate to Sarka, feeding the poor and ill 19. St Wenceslas being welcomed by Emperor Henry the Fowler (although Henry did not receive the title of Holy Roman Emperor, his son Otto I did, but because of Henry's importance he is referred to as Emperor in documents written in the times of his son, and St Wenceslas is referred to as 'King') 20. St Wenceslas receiving from Henry the relics of St Vitus and the title of King 21. St Wenceslas founding the rotunda of St Vitus 22. St Wenceslas freeing prisoners, unjustly kept in prison 23. St Wenceslas receiving Moravia under his rule, after Svatoboj has been expelled 24. St Wenceslas sending messengers to Rome 25. St Wenceslas visiting churches in winter with Podevin warming his feet in St Wenceslas's steps 26. Drahomira passing poisoned wine to St Wenceslas 27. St Wenceslas receiving holy communion and saying farewell before leaving for Boleslav's castle 28. In Boleslav's castle, a horse being made ready for St Wenceslas's escape, while the conspirators three times stand up ready to attack 29. St Wenceslas toasting St Michael 30. St Wenceslas being killed in front of the door of the Church of Saints Cosmas and Damian 31. Podevin being hanged 32. Christ revealing himself to King Erik of Denmark 33. Drahomira being swallowed by the earth for her sins 34. St Wenceslas restoring good health to Boleslav's wife, who suffered from fever and prayed to St Wenceslas for help 35. Pagans against the worship of St Wenceslas, being punished by lightning 36. The body of St Wenceslas being transferred from Stara Boleslav to Prague 37. St Wenceslas's ear, cut off during the assassination, being restored to his body; Hostivod receiving part of one of St Wenceslas's fingers 38. Sick people being cured beside the grave of St Wenceslas and a repentant Boleslav giving them alms 39. St Wenceslas ordering Boleslav to make coins with his picture 40. St Wenceslas ordering Henry of Moravia to go to Maria-Zell 41. St Wenceslas assisting the Czech King in a battle in 1260 42. King Vladislav II having a vision of Czech patron saints 43. Five verses of the St Wenceslas hymn 44. Ancestors of St Ludmila and Duke Borivoj.

Dr F. Stejskal who listed them in his book, published in 1929, also added that some elements of the legends, as they are shown in the above paintings, do not have precedent in the very old written legends. He lists these as pictures in chapels: 2, 3, 14, 18, 23, 24, 26, 27, 34, 35 and 39.

In 1929, as the millennium of St Wenceslas's death was celebrated, a major religious ceremony took place in Stara Boleslav. I remember my father telling me about the number of people who visited the basilica during those days and how he took part in a continuous 24 hour guard of honour beside the first grave of St Wenceslas in the crypt of the Church of Saints Cosmas and Damian.

The Church of Saint Mary, built outside the castle
In the year 1098, a new church was built in Stara Boleslav, dedicated to Saint Mary and Saint George. The church was built to the east of the castle where a large number of people already lived. But records are not available to shed more light on the whole history.

Another legend came to being in around 1160, in the reign of the Czech King Vladislav I, when a ploughman unearthed a metal picture of St Mary and the baby Jesus in his field just outside the Old Boleslav Castle. The legend tells us about the origin of this picture as it was passed verbally from generation to generation.

It is said that St Ludmila had her statues of pagan gods smelted, among them that of the goddess Krosina, which was made from pure gold, when the missionary St Methodius came to Bohemia after he had christened Duke Borivoj in Moravia. From the mixture of smelted metals, various instruments for Christian services were made. Among them was the picture of St Mary and the baby Jesus, which was consecrated by St Methodius and given to the Duchess Ludmila. She took it with her as a special gift to Tetin and worshipped it all her life and in fact met her death praying in front of it.

St Wenceslas inherited the picture from her and he too worshipped St Mary with the baby Jesus until the time of his death. Whenever St Wenceslas went for long journeys, the metal picture was carried in front of his knights, hanging on the top of a lance, according to eastern customs. It was frequently carried by his page Podevin.

Otherwise, the legend tells us, St Wenceslas carried the picture on his chest. The popular legend relates that Podevin hurriedly removed it from the chest of the dead Wenceslas on the morning of his murder, so it would not get into the hands of the assassins. As he was escaping, Podevin buried it in the field outside the castle, fearing that he might be caught. There it was unearthed by a ploughman, many years later, in around 1160.

A special legend is told about the finding of the picture. A farmer who was ploughing his field accidentally unearthed the picture. It happened apparently so: the farmer's oxen suddenly stopped at a specific spot, did not want go forward and started in fact to go backwards. The farmer stood there for a while, undecided, but then whipped his oxen to make them move forward. As the plough jerked forward, digging deeper into the soil, a metal picture was unearthed by the plough. It was a picture of St Mary and the baby Jesus. The farmer did not know who had buried it there and so he took it home. He was surprised to find it gone the next morning, but he unearthed it again in the field on the same spot. The same thing was repeated for two further nights and on the third morning he took the picture to the priests in the Basilica of St Wenceslas.

They put it in a safe place in the basilica, but to their surprise, the next morning it was again found in the field. The priests were puzzled by this but decided to build a small humble chapel (only 3m(10ft) x 2.5m(8ft) in size) in the field, on the same spot where the picture was originally unearthed. There it was placed on an altar and the local people came to pay their respects to the picture of St Mary and the baby Jesus, later referred to as 'Palladium'. Soon miraculous healings took place there according to legends, and people started to come in large numbers from distant places.

In 1617, the present large Baroque church was founded, with the help of Emperor Matthias and his wife, the Empress Anna, and collections from pilgrims. The architect chosen was an Italian, Jacob de Vaccani, who settled in Brandys.

Fig.13.8 Podevin carries Palladium in front of Wenceslas, after the victorious
duel with Radslav of Kourim - engraved in 1673 to Karel Skreta drawing

The new building absorbed the small chapel which still housed the Palladium of St Mary and the baby Jesus. The Thirty Years' War caused delays, but the main hall was finished in 1623.

On 5 December 1631 Saxony's army took Stara Boleslav, but it was not until February in the next year that the Austrian Imperial Army tried to retake Brandys and Stara Boleslav, where was an important crossing of the river Elbe. They were not successful. On 14 February 1632, the Palladium was stolen from the church by soldiers and on 24 February the whole church was looted and the interior was burnt. The soldiers passed the Palladium to Lieutenant Colonel Hoffkirch, an Austrian in the services of Saxony, then with their army in Prague.

He decided to humiliate the Palladium and on 29 March he put up gallows in the Old Town Square on which he hanged a carpentry apprentice. Opposite the gallows, on a chair, he nailed the Palladium. This proved unpopular with the people of Prague and he then hid the picture in his rooms at the house of the Italian born knight Antonio Binago.

On 15 May 1632 Prague was retaken by the Austrian Imperial Army and Saxony's army retreated to Germany. Hoffkirch withdrew to Leipzig. Another twist of fate happened, when in 1633 Hoffkirch's own brother, fighting on the Austrian side, was among seventeen officers executed for being cowards and for treason, on the same spot where the Palladium had been nailed to the chair on the Old Town Square in Prague.

It is believed that this was why Hoffkirch asked for such a high ransom - 95,000 ducats (gold coins) - for the return of the Palladium to Stara Boleslav. In the meantime the war continued and Stara Boleslav was occupied by the Swedish Army in 1634. It was then retaken by the Austrian Imperial soldiers. The war had a devastating effect on the local farming community. Fields were not sown for several years and there was great hunger among the people, who hid in the surrounding forests.

It was not until 1638 that the required sum of money was collected, including a large donation from Benigna Katerina of Lobkowicz. The Palladium was secretly returned to Prague, where it was placed in the Lobkowicz Palace. As the secret about the whereabouts of the Palladium became public knowledge, people petitioned the Emperor Ferdinand III, who was staying at that time in Prague Castle, for the return of the Palladium to Stara Boleslav.

The Emperor ordered the return of the picture and on 12 September 1638 at 2 p.m. a special procession left Hradcany, with priests carrying the Palladium on a stretcher, followed by Emperor Ferdinand and other noblemen and their wives and the people of Prague. They went across Prague, stopping in places and blessing the crowds lining the path of the procession. The Emperor and other noblemen and dignitaries then went ahead to Brandys, where a welcoming gate had been built in the town square. The procession arrived there by 9 p.m. and the Palladium was welcomed by the resident priests from Stara Boleslav.

Then under the light of torches they all went across the bridge over the river Elbe to Stara Boleslav. Special effects on the river Elbe were provided by students from Prague, who dressed as Neptune and other pagan gods, welcoming the Palladium and thus symbolising the conversion to Christianity. In Stara Boleslav, the path was lined by miners from the silver mines of Kutna Hora. They were dressed in their traditional costumes and their lamps lit the way for the procession.

In front of the Church of St Mary in Stara Boleslav, a large welcoming arch had been built and this was lined by students from Prague, dressed as angels. They had musical instruments and welcomed the procession with music and songs. People were moved by the joy and splendour and it is reported that the celebrations outdid those of many royal coronations.

The Palladium was placed on the main altar and the Dean of Stara Boleslav Chapter, Jiri Bilek, spoke to the people in Czech about the difficult years, when the Palladium was stolen and taken away from the church. Many people were moved to tears, including the Emperor. Afterwards, a small speech followed in Latin. Then the Prague students sang songs accompanied by musical instruments and the congregation was blessed.

It was not until then that the Emperor left for the castle at Brandys where he was to stay the night. However the congregation continued singing songs and praying throughout the whole night. The celebrations took place in a lull between fighting and so people hoped that there was to be an end to the war.

In 1639 Swedish units, under the leadership of Jan Banner started to move from North Germany towards Bohemia and soon occupied Stara Boleslav and Brandys, where they set up a camp for a time. One of the towers of the Basilica of St Wenceslas was demolished and the stone was used to make a raised platform for a gun. People had to leave their accommodation, as their houses were also demolished to form new fortifications in Stara Boleslav.

The churches were looted again but on 16 March 1632 the Palladium was taken for safe-keeping to Prague and then directly to Vienna to Emperor Ferdinand III and his Empress, who were both pleased to receive it. The Palladium was placed on an altar in their castle chapel and every day they prayed in front of it for the salvation of their country. Whenever they travelled, they took the Palladium with them in a specially decorated and adapted wagon. This wagon always led the convoy and the Emperor liked to say that Saint Mary, represented here by the Palladium, was the real Empress to be honoured.

When the imperial couple was expecting a family, the Empress asked for the Palladium to be brought into the bedroom and the future Emperor Leopold I was happily born in front of it on 9 June 1640. The Empress out of gratefulness had a special crown made for the Palladium from gold, diamonds and pearls.

The Empress would not let the Palladium leave her vicinity, and it stayed with her till her death on 13 May 1646. On her deathbed she admitted to her husband that she had had visions of Saint Mary asking her to return the Palladium to Stara Boleslav, and asked her husband to return it for her. The Emperor, after her death, took the Palladium to Prague, where on 5 August 1646, he had his first-born son

Ferdinand IV crowned as the Czech King. The Palladium was displayed in the St Wenceslas Chapel in St Vitus Cathedral and from there, on 19 August, was taken back to Stara Boleslav in a special procession, accompanied by people from Prague.

But the Thirty Years' War was not yet over and when there was a threat of the fighting moving back to Bohemia in 1648, the Palladium was moved to the Cathedral of St Vitus in Prague Castle, which was considered the safest place in Bohemia. After the battle of Augsburg, part of the Swedish Army under General Konigsmark went to Bohemia and by fast marches at night reached and entered Prague on the left-hand bank of the river Vltava. The Palladium was captured again, but the Swedish commandant, Karl Gustav, was persuaded by the daughter of Benigna of Lobkowicz, Anna Magdalen, wife of the Duke of Launenburg, to deliver the Palladium to the new Empress Marie Leopold in Vienna. He liked this idea, because he was currently negotiating for peace with the Austrian Emperor and the gift would help the matter.

In Prague, the Swedish soldiers attempted to take the part of Prague on the other side of the river Vltava, the Old Town and the New Town, but were beaten back by the residents in that part of Prague, the students and priests. Three days later came news about a peace treaty signed in Westphalia, by which the Thirty Years' War was ended. Many people at that time believed that the special powers of the Palladium helped to bring about the much needed peace.

The war was over, many people had died of hunger and Stara Boleslav was in ruins. Only St Mary's Church still stood. The Palladium was however still in Vienna. It was the Archbishop of Bohemia, Duke of Harrach and the Chancellor of the Kingdom of Bohemia who pleaded with the Emperor for the return of the Palladium. The Emperor agreed and the Palladium was first moved from the Emperor's Chapel to a church in Vienna, accompanied by priests, noblemen, and the crowned Czech King Ferdinand IV, also representing the Emperor who was ill at that time. The streets were lined by the people of Vienna. After a special service at the church, the Palladium left for Bohemia in a special convoy, guarded by the Emperor's soldiers.

The convoy reached Jindrichuv Hradec in Bohemia on 17 August 1650. People lined the route of the convoy and special welcoming celebrations were arranged in Hradec. After midnight on Saturday 20 August, the convoy reached Vysehrad in Prague, where the Palladium was displayed on the main altar of the Basilica of Saints Peter and Paul. The next day the Palladium was carried in a special procession across Prague to Prague Castle, where it was placed in the St Wenceslas Chapel. It left there on 6 September, with all the people of Prague lining the streets and a special service was held in the Church of St Benedict on the opposite side of the river. Next day the procession went all the way to Stara Boleslav.

The Palladium never left Bohemia again. It was twice moved from Stara Boleslav to be hidden, once in 1862, when the war with Turkey started, and once during the Second World War.

After the Thirty Years' War, Stara Boleslav was being rebuilt and one main tower was added to the Church of Saint Mary in 1670 costing 1642 gold coins. The other tower stood unfinished until the year 1749 when it was rebuilt at a cost of 4000 gold coins. The original old chapel housing the Palladium, which was on the left of the main altar, was retained until 1660, when it was demolished. Many pilgrims were disappointed over this hasty demolition of a very old holy place and complained. Count Stenberk arranged in 1672 for a new marble altar to be built on the same spot, and with a central painting depicting the legend about the Palladium being unearthed by a ploughman.

Many people and pilgrims visited Stara Boleslav and it was said that Stara Boleslav was the centre of Bohemia in a spiritual sense. Other Emperors came to Stara Boleslav too: Ferdinand I and II, Maximilian II, Rudolf II, Leopold I, Josef I, the Spanish King Carlos (24.9.1703), Karl VI, Marie Theresa, Josef II and Franz I. Carl the Last with his wife Zita came every day while they were staying in their castle in Brandys.

Stara Boleslav today

When I was growing up there, Stara Boleslav was a sleepy town. Between 1948, when the Communist Party was in control, and 1989, going to church was discouraged. This was especially true in the 50s and 60s and people were afraid to go to church, as it could cause them problems at work, or problems at school for their children. Once, when a cross with Jesus Christ was to be demolished by the authorities, my father saved it by moving it over the garden of St Wenceslas Basilica and placing it not far from the lion mentioned earlier.

My parents went to the church and so I was introduced to the story of St Wenceslas and how he forgave his brother as he was dying in Stara Boleslav. I have one photograph of me standing in the door to the Basilica of St Wenceslas. I was an altar boy there from the age of six. I remember that one teacher tried to make fun of me and my brother in front of the class, because we went to church. But otherwise, my childhood was happy; I had lots of friends and with the nearby river Elbe, lakes and forest, we had always plenty to do.

My parents wanted me to play the organ in church, so they saved up very hard to buy a piano for me, so I could start lessons. After a few years of lessons on the piano, I went for my first lesson to the Basilica of St Wenceslas, as the organ there was considered to be in better shape and repair than the one at St Mary's.

My teacher, the highly respected musician Josef Glazar, was very pleased with me at my first lesson. I continued practising for some time, but when I became fifteen and went to college, I gave up music, to the disappointment of my parents. I just did not believe I was talented enough.

In 1968, the year of the Prague Spring when, under the leadership of Alexander Dubcek, freedom started to flourish, I managed to get an invitation to Scotland, from a friend of Dr Vaclav Stepan from Stara Boleslav, himself a church-goer. My happy holiday in Britain was disrupted when the armies of the Warsaw Pact invaded Czechoslovakia. I was then fruit-picking in East Anglia. It was so unreal and so hard to take. It was some time before I got a letter from home advising me that they would telephone me on such and such a date. One month later, when we first spoke on the telephone, they wanted me to come home and I decided to return.

But on my return to Prague, as a student of the Technical University, the situation was very different to that during the days of Prague Spring before I left for my holiday. There was soon a one-week strike by all the students demanding the withdrawal of the occupying troops, but obviously without success. Then Jan Palach, a student, burnt himself on Wenceslas Square. It was not a happy time at all.

The situation was getting worse and for some time it was very confusing about the freedom of foreign travel. I managed to go on holiday to Britain again in the summer of 1969. An invitation was sent to me by Mr George Cansdale, who once in 1968 had helped me with accommodation, when I was looking for a hostel on Finchley Road in London, which was closed for redevelopment. It was later that I learned about his fame for his animal TV programmes on 'Blue Peter' and about his dedication to Christian work.

But the situation got worse in the summer of 1969 and the border around Czechoslovakia was soon permanently closed so I never returned. My parents, once in retirement, came to see me three times in nineteen years. The first time, my mother had to have a recommendation from her doctor, that she had to be accompanied by my father, because of her bad sight (and the doctor made it look worse), otherwise he would not have beeen allowed to go with her. It was in 1988 that I eventually returned to Czechoslovakia after nineteen years in Britain and spent a holiday with my parents. I also travelled around the historical places of the legends of St Wenceslas to fulfil my dream to write a book about these stories.

Since the Velvet Revolution of 1989, people in Bohemia and Moravia can now enjoy some of the basic freedoms, denied to them for so long. Life is a great deal happier there now, and people can freely visit the church, which is once more finding its place in society. The historic part of Stara Boleslav has been given new stone roads and pavements in the expectation of new visitors.

14. MELNIK

There are other places in the story of Good King Wenceslas which must not be missed. Some of them have been inhabited from the early days of mankind because of their geographical location like being near a river or stream, or on a hill which offered a natural defence against enemies.

Melnik is such a place, a hilltop site above the point where the river Vltava merges with the river Elbe. Archaeologial finds indicate an early settlement and then Celtic culture before the Slavonic people came. In the time of Wenceslas's grandmother Ludmila it was a fortified hilltop fort with wooden buildings. Through the centuries it developed into a mediaeval castle and then was rebuilt as a chateau. Today, it is surrounded by a town. The name Melnik is derived from the stone which forms the hill - arenaceous marl - which disintegrates when exposed to the weather, an effect which is translated in Czech as 'melni'.
The tribe from which Ludmila, a daughter of Slavibor, came was called Psovane. According to some historians, it originated from a group of Serbs who had settled

further north. Up to the present there has not been enough archaeological excavation to define the exact layout of the fortification during Ludmila's and Wenceslas's lives, but everything indicates that it lay within the boundaries of today's town and the dukal court was where the present castle - chateau - is. It is assumed that after the death of Duke Slavibor, the dukedom was inherited by Ludmila and, as she was married to Borivoj, it was added to the Premyslid Dukedom. Afterwards, the younger son of Borivoj, Vratislav, the father of Wenceslas also occupied the castle.

According to folk legends, Duchess Ludmila brought with her vine seedlings from Moravia and planted them on hilly ground near a village called Nedomice not far from Melnik. Even today, there is a strong vine-growing industry around Melnik and a white and a red wine are named after Duchess Ludmila.

In the Kristian's Legend, it is said that, as children Wenceslas and Boleslav stayed with their grandmother Ludmila in Melnik, but once Wenceslas took power, Melnik was given to his brother Boleslav to live in and administer. He however fortified a castle in Stara Boleslav, in the Roman way and moved there.

Duke Wenceslas still visited Melnik as one of his castles and as Kristian tells us: 'Wenceslas hurried to the vineyards, picked grapes and with his own hands quashed them, pouring the wine into jars and saving it for the holy service.' Thus the vineyard near Nedomice is even today called St Wenceslas Vineyard. The vineyard was neglected for some time, but more recently vines have been grown there again. There is a wine-cellar in the grounds of Old Boleslav Castle at which wine from St Wenceslas Vineyard is sold.

It was under Duke Boleslav II that the old wooden fort, referred to as Psov, was rebuilt and this new seat got the name 'civitas Melnic', where 'civitas' means 'village'. History tells us that Boleslav II's widow, Duchess Emma stayed there. She must have had a special position in the Holy Roman Empire, because she was the first duchess to mint her own coins. I was pleasantly surprised on my visit there to find that the local tourist office sold replicas of her coins. Duchess Emma also had the Gumpold Legend about Saint Wenceslas illuminated and the original is kept today in Wolfenbuttel in Germany. The title page has the illustration of Duchess Emma bowing in front of St Wenceslas.

Melnik was raised to the status of a royal town on 25 November 1274 by the Czech King Premysl Otakar II. After his death, it was his widow Kunhuta who occupied Melnik Castle.

Charles IV, the Czech King and Holy Roman Emperor, set up a special office in Melnik to protect the wine industry in the Melnik region. He brought new vines and methods to improve the local vine-growing industry from Burgundy, where he was brought up. He too had a vine named after him.

Fig. 14.1 Duchess Emma bowing in front of St Wenceslas

15. TETIN

Tetin was the place that Duchess Ludmila retired to. It was a fortification established on a hill near the river Berounka. Originally a wooden castle, it was rebuilt in stone during the reign of Wenceslas II, around the year 1288. It was destroyed during the Hussite Wars in 1422 and never rebuilt. I was told that the moat which separated the village from the former castle was filled in during the last century.

According to legends, it was the wooden church of St Michael which was built over the first grave of the Duchess Ludmila. This was rebuilt in stone in the Romanesque style around 1225. It was converted to the Baroque style in 1836. The dedication was changed to St Jan of Nepomuk in around 1603. The church is surrounded by a small cemetery.

Another small church, still standing today in the former castle grounds is the church dedicated to St Catherine, established in 1200. (See fig. 15.1.) It originally served for knights who had returned from missions to recover the Holy Land. Later it was used as a general store but it was renovated and returned to church use in 1858, when a small tower was added.

Yet another church was built in the grounds of the castle, and was consecrated to St Ludmila (see fig. 15.2.) at the end of the 17th century. Under the altar there is a special pebble stone (see fig. 15.3.), on which the Duchess Ludmila used to kneel and pray, and the folk legend tells that this was how she met her death.

Except a few stones from the castle wall remaining at the far end of the former castle grounds, there is nothing left of the castle. People in the village of Tetin have used the stone from the castle to build their houses.

16. STOCHOV

Stochov is, according to folk legends, the birthplace of Good King Wenceslas. The oaktree which still stands there today is clearly very old, but no dating of it has been possible which might prove the folk legends. Stochov may not have been a large fortification. It is situated on a small hill and today there are some buildings with walls still left from the very old days. I was told that when people dig deep to form foundations for new houses, they very often come across stones and debris from the old days.

I am not aware that proper archaeological excavations have ever been made in Stochov which might prove that it was a fortification at the time of Prince Wenceslas's birth. However, except for the folk legends, there is no mention in the written legends, of the place of Wenceslas's birth. In Stochov, there is a church dedicated to St Wenceslas, supporting the claim that it was the birthplace of Prince Wenceslas. (See fig. 16.1 and 16.2.) I personally believe the folk legend about Stochov being the birthplace of Prince Wenceslas, because there is no other reason why such a legend would have been created about an otherwise unimportant settlement.

17. LIBUSIN

Libusin is believed to be the place at which Duchess Libuse pronouced her vision of Prague becoming a famous castle and city, from which the two famous saints, St Wenceslas and St Adalbert would come. But we know that Cosmas already knew the history of the two saints when he was writing his chronical.

Archaeologists indeed excavated the site, trying to find clues supporting the legend about Libuse. Finds indicate that there was a village settlement which could have existed in her time (6th-7th century), but the hope of finding her grave was not fulfilled. An object found during the excavations, a plate with an engraved sun with its rays, suggests that the place could have been the site of pagan rituals. However, the fortifications constructed at the end of the 9th century destroyed most of the village that had existed before, making any further archaeological studies impossible. By the 11th century the castle had fallen into disrepair and was forgotten. Only the church with its cemetery, has been maintained throughout the centuries to the present day. (See fig. 17.1.)

Today, the site is covered by a meadow. The present church dates from much later days, and probably replaced the original wooden church. The first mention of it was in the 14th century. It was the place where Prince Wenceslas would have been christened, assuming the folk legend about his birth in Stochov is true.

18. BUDEC

Budec is also placed on a hill and, as in Libusin, only the church now remains from the original castle where young Prince Wenceslas was once sent by his father Duke Vratislav for his education.

Budec is mentioned in the First Slavonic Legend, written around 940, where it is said: 'Grandmother Ludmila had Wenceslas educated in reading Slovanic books by her priest. Wenceslas understood the Slavonic books well. Vratislav, his father, then took him to Budec, where the boy learned to read Latin books. He also learned Latin well.'

In the Second Slavonic Legend, it is said that Spytihnev established a church dedicated to St Peter in Budec. It is also said that: 'This boy [Wenceslas], who was unusually bright and of attractive looks, when he reached the first period of his flowering youth [about 12 years], while his father was still alive, and as he was very keen to educate himself, he convinced his father so he sent him to the castle called Budec, to the priest called Uceno [Ucenus in Latin], to learn reading and writing.'

Archaeological excavations have proved that there was a school. Fragments were found of plates, which were covered in wax and then written on using a sharp metal instrument, called a 'stilus'. The wax was then smoothed with the flat end of the stilus so it could be used again.

The Church of St Peter in Budec, established by Duke Spytihnev in around 895-905, is still there in its original structure. We can say that this is the only building still standing in Bohemia which the young Prince Wenceslas must have entered - the church where he knelt and prayed. (See fig. 18.1 and 18.2.)

Archaeological excavations have not only unearthed the foundations of another church, which was dedicated to St Mary, but have also indicated that the hill was first inhabited as early as the late Bronze Age. But beyond the information about Budec being the place of education of the young Wenceslas in the 10th century, history does not tell us much about what happened afterwards. From a document signed by Queen Kunhuta in 1262, in which she transferred the administration of the church with all that was in Budec, to the Chapter of Vysehrad, we can deduce that by this time the castle had already fallen into disrepair. The stone may have been used for other buildings in villages below the fortification and only the land remained. The original fortification was on a site of 80 hectares, which for those days was very large.

Later history mentions the Church of Saints Peter and Paul on a regular basis. It is still in use today and a holy mass is served there every last Sunday of the summer months. The cemetery around the church is still used and contains the graves of several famous writers, artists and priests. On a Sunday close to the feast of St Wenceslas, on 28 September, a special pilgrimage was made to Budec each year, a custom which was interrupted after the Second World War, but was re-established in 1992.

19. LEVY HRADEC

Levy Hradec is the oldest seat of the Czech Dukes. From a very old legend called 'Short writings about Saints Cyril and Methodius' it is described how Methodius christened Borivoj and his 30 people in Moravia at the court of Svatopluk. For Borivoj's journey back, Methodius gave him a priest called Kaich. When Borivoj returned to his castle, called Hradec, he made a home there for the priest and he also built a church dedicated to St Clement.

Once Borivoj built his castle in Prague, Levy Hradec gradually lost importance. But it was still used for the election in 982 of the second bishop of Prague - Vojtech - later known as Saint Adalbert. And although it was no longer a ducal seat, it has continued to be linked to the origins of Christianity in Bohemia.

The excavations of the site indicate early settlements from Neolithic times through the Bronze Age to the Slavonic fortifications of the Czech tribe. But the castle fell into disrepair and today there are fields and meadows with some indication in the terrain of the various fortifications, ramparts and moats.

From the reconstruction (fig 19.1) the site was quite large and in two parts. At times of danger, inhabitants from the surrounding villages sought sanctuary there for themselves and their farm animals. Yet again we can see that only the Church of Saint Clement continued to be maintained throughout the centuries. (See fig. 19.2.) As recently as 1940, during repairs to the building the foundations of Borivoj's rotunda were found underneath the present church. Thus the legends about the first church in Bohemia were confirmed.

20. BLANIK

Blanik has a very special place in this book. The first part of the book ends with the folk legend of St Wenceslas and Blanik's Knights. There really is a mountain called Blanik in Bohemia and at one time there was a castle on top of it. Its early history falls as far as Celtic times and there was a Celtic fort too. St Wenceslas has been important to the Czech people throughout the centuries, and has always been the saint they have prayed to for help. At times their prayers have been answered and they have defended their kingdom. I have no doubt that in mediaeval times the story really was believed. When the Czech national revival occurred, still under the Austrian Empire, it was the priests who led the way, and thus we find the painting of the immortal St Wenceslas leading Blanik's Knights, just above the site of Duke Wenceslas's death in Stara Boleslav.

Today one can walk up the Blanik mountain, and a key can be borrowed in the village Lounovice below the mountain for the viewing tower. One can also look around from the tower. Once, as I walked down from the mountain, I stumbled over a stone and when I picked it up I saw on it shiny grains. I puzzled over it, but then, knowing my luck, I threw it away. On the way back we stopped with friends at the castle of Konopiste. There I looked at the regional map and saw that there was once a gold mine on the other side of Blanik, in the last century. Maybe I will be more lucky the next time I go there. (See fig. 20.1, 20.2 and 20.3.)

21. RINGSTED IN DENMARK AND AACHEN IN GERMANY

I once travelled to Denmark to look for the Church of Saint Wenceslas, which according to the Czech legend was built there by King Erik. I found King Erik's grave in Ringsted but more research will be required to clarify this legend.

I also visited Aachen in Germany. This was the place where the Czech King and Emperor Charles IV had an altar of St Wenceslas established in the cathedral on 3 December 1362. This altar was replaced by another altar, around 1453-7, provided by Sigismund of Jihlava, a Canon from Stara Boleslav. The new altar now hangs in the Treasury. (See fig. 21.1.) Saint Wenceslas is in the middle section on the left, recommending the kneeling Emperor and Czech King Charles IV to Jesus Christ. On the right of the middle section are St John and St Vitus, recommending the kneeling Ladislav Posthumous, King of Bohemia and Hungary, to Jesus Christ.

On the outer wings are: on the left, St Sigismund and St Ludmila; and on the right, St Adalbert and St Prokopius. The paintings are to express hope in the continuation of the Bohemian Royal dynasty. In Aachen there is also a church dedicated to St Adalbert. The Polish King Boleslav Chrabry sent relics of St Adalbert to Emperor Otto III, who ruled from Aachen. The church (see fig. 21.2.) was then established in Aachen to house the relics of St Adalbert, a friend and advisor to Otto III.

Fig. 1.2   Ploughman Premysl (in the centre) with two of Libuse's messengers
- a wall painting in a rotunda in Znojmo, Moravia

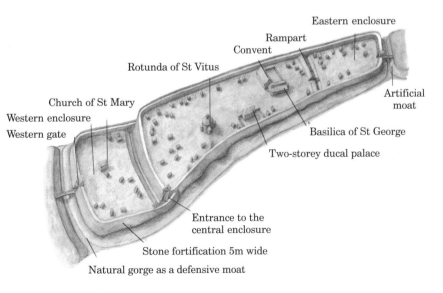

Fig. 2.1   Prague Castle in the late 10th century (by L. Anlauf)

Fig. 2.2 The birth of Wenceslas - painting in Stara Boleslav

Fig. 2.3   The thousand-year-old oaktree in today's Stochov

Fig. 3.1   Ludmila teaches Wenceslas (an altar painting in Tetin)

Fig. 3.2 Young Wenceslas works in the field and in the vineyards

65

Fig. 3.3 St Michael's Church in Tetin, now dedicated to St John of Nepomuk

Fig. 4.   Prince Wenceslas is enthroned

Fig. 4.2   Wenceslas with priests as his advisors, in contrast to Drahomira
persecuting priests on the right and presiding over a pagan gathering

67

Fig. 4.2.1 Wenceslas after the duel with Duke Radslav

Fig. 4.2.2 Wenceslas buying children out of slavery (on the right)
and providing a shelter for orphans (on the left)

Fig. 4.2.3 Helmet, iron shirt and sword held in St Vitus Treasury, reportedly belonging to Wenceslas. The sword was later used in the Chapel of St Wenceslas during coronations of Czech kings in the ceremony for creating Knights of St Wenceslas (Photo: Dr Stejskal)

Fig. 4.3   Good King Wenceslas delivers wood to a widow - from a painting in Stara Boleslav

69

Fig. 4.4 Consecration of St Vitus Rotunda

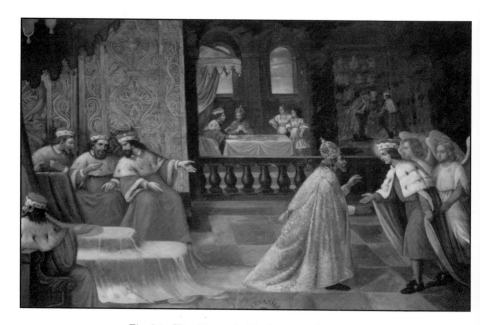

Fig. 6.1 King Henry the Fowler greets Wenceslas

Fig. 6.2   Considering going to Rome and passing the rule to Boleslav

Fig. 8.1   Murder of Good King Wenceslas, as illustrated in Gumpold's Legend

Fig. 8.2   Murder of Good King Wenceslas (by L. Kohl in 1789)

Fig.10.4   John Mason Neale and family at Sackville College in 1855

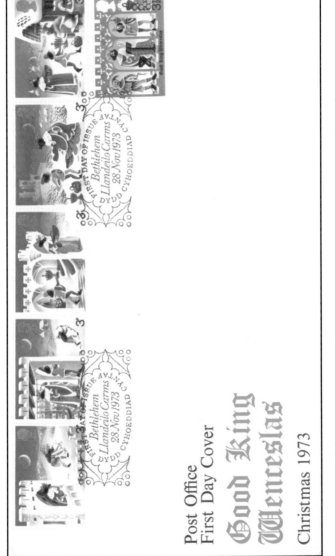

Fig.10.5 British Christmas stamps, First Day Cover 1973 (shown 75% of actual size)

Fig.11.1 Part of a sculpture on the door of St Vitus Cathedral, depicting, at the top, St Wenceslas leading Blanik's Knights

74

Fig.11.3   Details of the sculptures in Stara Boleslav

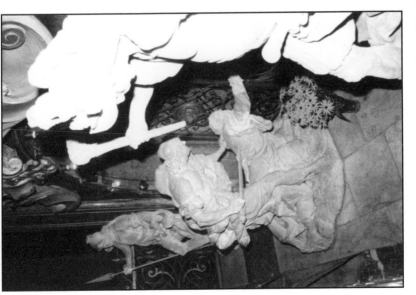

Fig.11.2   Place of martyrdom of Saint Wenceslas in Stara Boleslav; statues depicting the act while the painting above shows the immortal St Wenceslas leading Blanik's Knights

75

Fig.12.2   St Vitus Cathedral today

Fig.12.3   Prague Castle today from Petriny Tower

Fig.12.4   The foundations of St Mary's Church (Photo: Ivan Borkovsky)

Fig.12.5 St George Basilica from the tower of St Vitus Cathedral

Fig.12.7   Statue of St Wenceslas - his closest depiction (Copyright SPH)

79

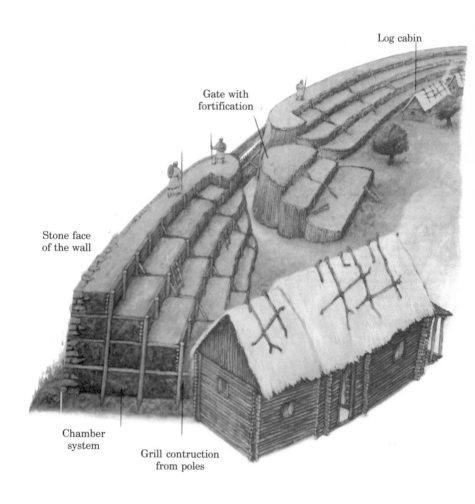

Log cabin

Gate with
fortification

Stone face
of the wall

Chamber
system

Grill contruction
from poles

Fig.12.8   Artist's reconstruction of a typical fortification (by L. Anlauf)

Fig.12.9 Prague Castle in 1572. Engraving by F. Hoogenberghe

Fig.12.11 The first statue of St Wenceslas in Horse Market (later Wenceslas Square)
by Jan J. Bendl. Painting by Josef Carmine in 1785

Fig.12.11.1 View of the Horse Market from the Horse Gate in 1835,
painting by Vincenc Morstadt

Fig.12.12 The present statue of St Wenceslas, surrounded by four Czech saints:
Agnes, Ludmila, Procopius and Adalbert (hidden behind the structure)

Fig.13.1 Engraving of Stara Boleslav from 1822, 1.Basilica of St Wenceslas (centre) 2. Church of Saint Mary (on the left)
3. Castle walls from the time of Charles IV (centre) 4.East gate (centre left) 5. Castle in Brandys (on the right)

Fig.13.2 View inside St Wenceslas Basilica

Fig.13.3 View inside the Crypt of Saints Cosmas and Damian,
with the first grave of St Wenceslas in the middle

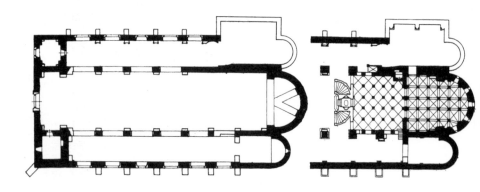

Fig.13.4 Drawings of the basilica and the crypt

Fig.13.5 Statue of a lion where the emperor's throne once stood

Fig.13.6 Archaeological dig along the walls of Old Boleslav Castle

Fig.13.7 A chapel on the route from Prague to
Stara Boleslav, one of the original forty-four

Fig.13.9 Chapel of Blessed Podevin, in the place
where he was hanged in Stara Boleslav

88

Fig.13.10 Podevin removing Palladium from the chest of the murdered Wenceslas (centre right)

Fig.13.11 The unearthing of Palladium - a painting on an altar above the actual place in St Mary's Church

Fig.13.12 Palladium - St Mary with the Baby Jesus

Fig.13.13 Church of St Mary in Stara Boleslav

Fig.13.14 The interior of St Mary's Church

Fig.14.2 Melnik Castle today with the Church of Saints Peter and Paul on the right

Fig.15.1 Churches of St Catherine and St Ludmila in Tetin

Fig.15.2 Church of St Ludmila in Tetin

Fig.15.3 Inside the Church of St Ludmila - the pebble stone on which St Ludmila knelt during her prayers is kept behind glass doors under the altar

Fig.16.1 Church of St Wenceslas in Stochov

Fig.16.2 Inside the church in Stochov

Fig.17.1 Church of St George with its cemetery, in the grounds of the former Libusin Castle

Fig.18.1 Church of St Peter in Budec, now also dedicated to St Paul

Fig.18.2 Inside the small Budec church, where floor tiles indicate the location of the original altar

97

Fig.18.3 Children running down the rampart in Budec

Fig.19.1 Reconstruction of Levy Hradec, which was situated on the left bank of the river Vltava

Fig.19.2 The present Church of St Clement

Fig.19.3 The foundations of the rotunda of St Clement
underneath the present church (by Ivan Borkovsky)

Fig 19.4 Rotunda of St Clement (Painting by L. Anlauf)

Fig.20.1 Blanik mountain from a distance

Fig.20.2 Viewing tower on top of Blanik

Fig.20.3 Stone, where castle walls once stood on top of Blanik

Fig.21.1 St Wenceslas altar in Aachen Cathedral Treasury

Fig.21.2 Church of St Adalbert in Aachen

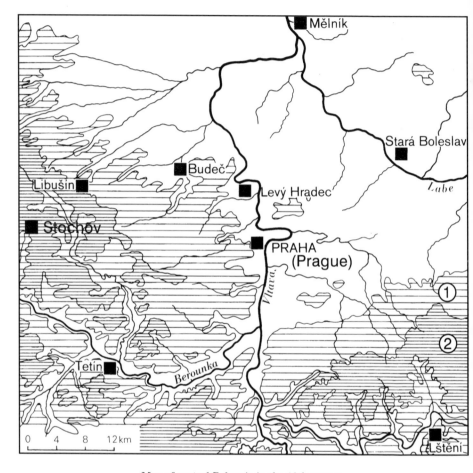

Map of central Bohemia in the 10th century

1. 300 metres above sea level
2. 400 metres above sea level